Leading the board

Leading the board

The six disciplines of world-class chairmen

Andrew Kakabadse
and
Nada Kakabadse

First published in 2008 by
PALGRAVE MACMILLAN
Houndmills, Basingstoke, Hampshire RG21 6XS and
175 Fifth Avenue, New York, N.Y. 10010
Companies and representatives throughout the world

PALGRAVE MACMILLAN is the global academic imprint of the Palgrave Macmillan division of St. Martin's Press, LLC and of Palgrave Macmillan Ltd. Macmillan® is a registered trademark in the United States, United Kingdom and other countries. Palgrave is a registered trademark in the European Union and other countries.

ISBN-13: 978–0–230–53684–5
ISBN-10: 0–230–53684–0

This book is printed on paper suitable for recycling and made from fully managed and sustained forest sources. Logging, pulping and manufacturing processes are expected to conform to the environmental regulations of the country of origin.

A catalogue record for this book is available from the British Library.

A catalog record for this book is available from the Library of Congress.

10 9 8 7 6 5 4 3 2 1
17 16 15 14 13 12 11 10 09 08

Printed and bound in China

*To Alexei Mordashov, the Severstal Organisation
and the Severstal Board*
                                        May you grow and prosper

Contents

Contents

FIGURES

Tables

ACKNOWLEDGMENTS

We would like to thank all of those who have, over the last five years, generously given their time to be interviewed as part of our research. In particular we would like to thank (alphabetically) those we quote in the text:

Aclan Acar, chief executive officer, Doğus Otomotiv, Turkey

Ishak Alaton, chairman and founder, Alarko Holdings, Turkey

Tony Alexander, non executive director and deputy chairman, Imperial Tobacco Group plc; former UK chief operating officer and director of Hanson plc; former chairman of Marley plc; non executive director of Misys plc; Inchcape plc, Cookson Group plc, Laporte plc, United Kingdom

Don Argus, chairman, BHP Billiton, Australia

George Bell, chairman, Anglia Farmers, United Kingdom

John Berndt, member and former chairman, Thunderbird Board of Trustees, United States of America

Len Bleasel, chairman, ABN Amro Australia Holdings Pty Limited; member of the Advisory Council, ABN Amro Australia Pty Limited, Australia

Derek Bonham, former chairman, Imperial Tobacco Group plc, United Kingdom

Lord Sandy Bruce-Lockhart, leader of Kent County Council, United Kingdom

Lord Terry Burns, chairman, Marks and Spencer; chairman, Abbey National; chairman, Welsh Water, United Kingdom

Sir Colin Chandler, chairman, easyJet plc, United Kingdom

Michael Chaney, chairman, National Australia Bank, Australia

David Clarke, chairman, Macquarie Bank, Australia

Peter Cummings, chief executive, Bank of Scotland Corporate, United Kingdom

Viscount Etienne Davignon, Minister of State; chairman of CMB, Recticel; vice chairman Suez-Tractebel, Belgium

Kate Davies, CEO, Notting Hill Housing Trust, United Kingdom

Gareth Davis, CEO, Imperial Tobacco Group plc, United Kingdom

Rosalind Gilmore, chairman, Leadership Foundation, Washington DC; former independent director, Zurich Financial Services, Switzerland

Lord Clive Hollick, partner, Kohlberg Kravis Roberts & Co; senior director, Diageo plc; director, Honeywell Inc; chairman, SBS Broadcasting; chairman, South Bank Centre, United Kingdom

Nick Johnson, chief executive officer, Bexley Council, United Kingdom

Lady Barbara Thomas Judge, chairman of the United Kingdom Atomic Energy Authority, United Kingdom

Ronnie Kells, chairman, United Drug, Ireland

Vadim Makhov, chairman, Severstal North America; former chairman of Russian and European companies; director of Corporate Strategy, Severstal Group, Russia

Susan R. Meisinger, J.D., SPHR, president and CEO, Society for Human Resource Management (SHRM), United States of America

Pat Molloy, former chairman, CRH; chairman, Enterprise Ireland; chairman, Blackrock Clinic, Ireland

Herbert Müller, CEO, Ernst & Young, Germany

Professor Helen G. Nellis, MA, barrister, former chairman, Bedfordshire and Luton Health Authority; chairman, Bedford Hospitals NHS Trust, United Kingdom

Maurice L. Newman AC, chairman, Australian Securities Exchange, Australia

G. Kelly O'Dea, chairman, AllianceHPL Worldwide; chairman, Outward Bound International, United States of America

James G. Parkel, past president of American Association of Retired Persons (AARP), United States of America

Sir John Parker, chairman, National Grid plc; senior non executive director (chair) Bank of England, United Kingdom

Eric Parsons, chairman, president, and CEO, Standard Insurance Company, United States of America

John Phillips, chairman, Foreign Investment Review Board, Australia

Jeremy Pope, chairman, Milklink, United Kingdom

David Pumphrey, partner, Heidrick & Struggles, Australia

Bernard G. Rethore, chairman emeritus, Flowserve Corporation; chairman, McDyre & Spendley Ltd, United States of America

Major General (Ret) Stephen Rippe, USA executive vice president and chief operating officer, Protestant Episcopal Cathedral Foundation, United States of America

Lord Tom Sawyer, chancellor of University of Teesside; former chairman, The Labour Party; former chairman, Notting Hill Housing Trust, United Kingdom

Dr Bernd Scheifele, CEO/president, Heidelberg Cement, Germany

Lord Dennis Stevenson of Coddenham, chairman, HBOS plc; former chairman Pearson plc, United Kingdom

Vannie Treves, UK chairman, Korn Ferry International; chairman, Intertek Group Plc; chairman, Equitable Life; chairman, National College of School Leadership

Ellen Van Velsor, senior fellow, Center for Creative Leadership, United States of America

Ray Webster, former CEO, easyJet, United Kingdom

Thanks in particular to Lord Tom Sawyer of Darlington; Kate Donaghy of Manchester Square Partners, the United Kingdom; David Pumphrey of Heidrick & Struggles, Australia; Ellen Van Velsor of the Center for Creative Leadership, the United States; Keith Niblett, Thunderbird School of Global Management, the United States; Dr Robert Galavan, National University of Ireland, Maynooth, Ireland; Orhan Yavuz of SCMC, Turkey; and Andreas Schnurr, Heidelberg Cement, Germany for their enthusiastic help in organizing interviews with some of the most fascinating business and public service leaders in both the northern and southern hemispheres.

Our deepest gratitude to Alex Kessler for typing script after script of sometimes unintelligible text and to Sheena Darby. A special mention must also be made of two outstanding editors, Stuart Crainer and Des Dearlove, whose wizardry with words has brought this book to life.

Finally, this book and so many other studies would not have been possible without the generosity and forethought of the top management of the Severstal Corporation. We are deeply indebted to Alexei Mordashov, Vadim Makhov, Vadim Shvetsov, Anatoly Kruchinin, Mikhail Noskov, Dmitry Afanasyev, and Dmitry Kouptsov for their funding and encouragement to research and dig deep so that others may benefit.

This book is a tribute to you all.

ANDREW KAKABADSE
AND
NADA KAKABADSE

Andrew Kakabadse (a.p.kakabadse@cranfield.ac.uk) is Professor of International Management Development at Cranfield University's School of Management in the United Kingdom. He holds, and has also held, visiting appointments at the Centre for Creative Leadership and Thunderbird, The Garvin School of International Management, in the United States; at the University of Ulster in the United Kingdom; at the Australian Graduate School of Entrepreneurship, Swinburne University of Technology, Australia; and at Macquarie Graduate School of Management, Australia. Andrew has consulted and lectured in every region of the world. His bestselling books include *The Politics of Management, Working in Organizations,* and *The Wealth Creators.*

Nada Kakabadse (Nada.Kakabadse@Northampton.ac.uk) is a research professor at the University of Northampton Business School in the United Kingdom. Previously, she was a senior research fellow at the Cranfield School of Management. Nada has worked for international organizations in Scandinavia, the Middle East, and North Africa, as well as for the Canadian Federal Government and the Australian Public Services Department of Employment, Education, and Training.

Andrew and Nada are the authors of eight books: *Leadership in Government* (1998); *Essence of Leadership* (1999); *Creating Futures: Innovative Applications of IS/IT* (2000); *The Geopolitics of Governance* (2001); *Smart Sourcing* (2002); *Intimacy* (2004); *Governance, Strategy, and Policy* (editors, 2006); and *CSR in Practice* (2007).

In recent years, vociferous public debate and an ocean of ink have been devoted to the subject of corporate governance. In part, we have Enron and a handful of other corporate wrong-doers to thank for that. In the United States, a string of very public corporate scandals led Congress to pass the Sarbanes–Oxley Act, beefing up the rules and regulations that boards have to comply with. Sarbanes–Oxley ushered in a new era of account-ability in American boardrooms. If we were in any doubt, it re-underlined the importance of the board in corporate affairs in the twenty-first century.

So, who leads the board of directors in a modern corporation? It is a simple enough question. The correct answer, of course, is the chairman, but members of the public could be excused for getting it wrong. Well intentioned as it was, Sarbanes-Oxley – and a great deal of the media coverage surrounding it – focused on the role of the chief executive officer (CEO) and, to a lesser extent, on that of the chief financial officer (CFO). By com-parison, very little attention was lavished on the role of the chairman.

Why was this? The CEO and CFO are seen as the leader and the financial controller, respectively. Leadership and money have an understandable and perennial allure. But the notion that the CEO is the leader rather than the chairman is actually a rela-tively recent – and largely mistaken – development. Up until about 30 years ago, the chairman role was regarded as the senior cor-porate position. It is only now making a comeback, but it is a comeback that will continue to gather pace and which will have repercussions for those who work as chairmen and for all who interact with boards.

In many firms, especially in the United States, of course, the job titles of CEO and chairman are held by the same person, a fact that partly explains the confusion. This combination of titles is, in our opinion, misleading and potentially dangerous in terms of both governance and corporate performance. Being a chairman and being a CEO are fundamentally different roles.

So, while all the evidence and research points to the importance of an effective well-led board, the one role that has been largely neglected is the most important of all: that of the chairman. Put simply, without an effective chairman there cannot be an effective board. And, even when you have a great CEO who is also the chairman, their CEO skills are not sufficient on their own to ensure a well-led board. We believe it is high time this fact was acknowledged.

An additional confusion is semantics. The title "chairman" has an old fashioned, clearly male ring to it. It conjures up images of mahogany board tables and whisky sours over genial chitchat. Though it comes laden with baggage, it is the word we are stuck with. Chairwoman is now rarely used, despite the increasing numbers of women in chair roles. If we were to start again, we would suggest *chair-leader* as a title, but for the purposes of this book we refer throughout to chairmen.

Our argument and research

The central argument behind *Leading the Board* is twofold. First, that the role of the chairman is distinct from that of anyone else on the board or elsewhere in the organization, requiring its own unique set of skills and qualities. And second, that the role of the chairman as the leader of the board of directors, is the most critical one of all for the long term success of the firm. In short, world-class companies require world-class chairmen.

So what should we look for in a world-class chairman? That is the simple question that has driven our research for the past years. The comments quoted in this book are recent, gathered over the last eighteen months. However, the full programme of study is extensive. That research, which now extends to top teams and to boards covering more than 12,000 organizations in 17 countries, including 400 board members, has convinced us of four important points.

First, some elements of the chairman role transcend national boundaries. Despite cultural, legal, and political differences between countries, and irrespective of differences in board structure, our research indicates that there is a meaningful set of skills and qualities that denote world-class chairmen. Again and again, people talked about the "disciplines of the chairman." And the same six disciplines applied whether he or she was operating in Tokyo or Toledo, New York or New Delhi, Moscow or Madrid.

Second, the role of the chairman today is largely misunderstood and undervalued. This is despite the fact that the chairman was traditionally the preeminent corporate role. What has happened over the past 40 or so years is an elevation of the CEO role to that of corporate hero. This has clearly diminished the role of the chair. In the past, the chairman role was recognized as the one that handled the contradictions and ambiguities, balancing the interests of the company's employees, executives, customers, and shareholders. The CEO is now seen as carrying out this juggling act. It is no coincidence that this lionization of the CEO has been most pronounced in North America, where the dual role of CEO and chairman is common.

Third, and linked to the previous point, there is very little formal training and development for directors taking on the position of chairmen. Traditionally, new chairmen have had to make the transition by developing themselves. Nor have business schools and other external training suppliers developed effective programs for new chairmen. If boards are to become more effective – and more Enrons are to be avoided – there is an urgent need to find ways of supporting the development of chairmen.

Finally, the current quality of chairmen varies greatly – even within countries. One of the most alarming research findings is the variable quality of chairman in US companies. On the one hand, the best American companies have world-class chairmen. Yet, on the other, in the vast majority of US firms, the quality of the chairmen is mediocre at best. This is a serious challenge facing corporate America. The situation in other countries including those of Western Europe is slightly better but still requires urgent attention.

Other significant findings from our research are as follows:

- Three-quarters of boards do not know how they contribute value.
- There is a culture of inhibition in American boardrooms as a result of role duality and oppressive legislation. This is fostering a conspiracy of silence in US boardrooms.
- Board structure and formal governance regulations are less important in preventing governance breaches and corporate wrongdoing than the culture and trust created by chairmen.

About the book

This book is our attempt to bring some clarity to the role of the chairman in the twenty-first century.

The Introduction chapter examines the modern role of the chairman and how it came about, including the current confusion surrounding it. It also identifies the six disciplines of world-class chairmen: delineating boundaries; sense making; interrogating the argument; influencing outcomes; living the values; and developing the board. The next six chapters examine each of these disciplines in turn.

The second chapter titled "Discipline 1: delineating boundaries" states that the role of the chairman must be distinct from that of the board and distinct also from that of the CEO and management. One of our interviewees argued that boards exist to appoint management, oversee performance, and enable management to improve performance. There are, however, many other possible roles for the board. Moreover, it is critical to think about who serves on the board. It is only by clearly delineating boundaries between roles that the board – and the chairman – hold that allows both to effectively function.

The third chapter titled "Discipline 2: sense making" declares that chairmen must communicate and champion the organization's mission, values, and strategy so that they resonate with an array of internal and external audiences. For a chairman, this sense making has two aspects: the use of logic and the use of chemistry. Chairmen must excel at both.

The fourth chapter titled "Discipline 3: interrogating the argument" states that a key role of a board is to interrogate management about its strategy and policy. Managers should know how to submit ideas and reports to a board. Boards should decide if they want to consider proposals by dialogue or by debate. It falls to the chairman to ensure that the discussion remains constructive.

The fifth chapter titled "Discipline 4: influencing outcomes" declares that sometimes a chairman can do more by influencing decisions than issuing commands, harnessing opinion to gain enthusiastic support for a particular outcome. There are five steps toward effective influencing: surfacing sentiments, working through divisions, using judicious speech, focusing on the most salient points, and scheduling meetings to align everyone's expectations.

The sixth chapter titled "Discipline 5: living the values" asserts that trust and integrity are critical to chairmen and to boards. For the chairman it is important to be aware of the ethics and values challenges confronting a board. There are espoused values and values actually practiced. An imbalance can be a problem for any chairman.

The seventh chapter titled "Discipline 6: developing the board" declares that every board and every chairman needs to be developed. This can be either a very formal or a very informal process. Development starts with a process for assessment and review. How to develop the chairman is a special and demanding topic – there are some 40 criteria that need to be measured.

Finally, in "On being world class: the six disciplines at work," we pull it all together to examine what it means to be a world-class chairman. Drawing on their own experiences, senior executives and chairmen discuss the six disciplines in practice.

Each chapter is filled with insights from our research interviews with chairmen throughout the world. These serve as reality checks on how the theory stands up to the messy reality and the challenges that face chairmen on a daily basis.

The rise, fall, and rise of the chairman

> The chairman is in the pivotal position. The culture of the company starts with the chairman.
> Lady Barbara Thomas Judge, Chairman,
> United Kingdom Atomic Energy Authority

"Pivotal" is a good word to describe the role of the chairman in the modern organization.[1] In military terminology, pivotal describes the person or people about whom a body of troops wheels when it changes direction. As the leader of the board of directors, the chairman fulfills that role in the corporation. He or she is responsible for ensuring that the firm is legally, morally, and commercially on track.

In recent years, too, the burden on boards has increased as a host of new pressures have been brought to bear. These include new governance legislation, such as Sarbanes–Oxley in the United States; voluntary codes from securities commissions; stock exchange listing requirements; and increasing pressure from investor associations and even major world bodies, such as the Organization for Economic and Co-operative Development (OECD). As a result, boards of companies are increasingly accountable for:

- the defense of shareholders' rights;
- the monitoring of management;
- the accuracy, timeliness, and transparency of financial and nonfinancial reporting;
- the defence of the reputation of the company;
- the long-term prosperity of the firm;
- risk assessment and management.[2]

As the responsibilities heaped on boards mount, sound leadership becomes even more vital. It is the chairman who must provide that leadership. Little wonder then that Barbara Thomas Judge, an internationally accomplished lawyer, experienced board director and chairman of one of the most controversial organizations in the United Kingdom (dealing with atomic energy), describes the role as "pivotal."

Who's in charge?

Yet, despite the obvious importance of the chairman, the role has received surprisingly little attention. Witness the many books on the role of the CEO compared to a handful on the chairman. One reason for this is that it is not clear who is in charge of the corporation. For many people, the role of corporate leader has become synonymous with the CEO. In the United States, this is partly due to the common practice of combining the CEO and chairman roles. To some extent this has simplified a difficult distinction. It has also had the negative effect of avoiding the issue by blurring the two roles into one. That issue must now be confronted.

The lionizing of CEOs can be witnessed simply by looking at magazine covers. Thirty or so years ago, CEOs were not recognized when they walked down the street. Who were the CEOs of General Electric before Jack Welch? Who led the two companies which were molded into ABB before Percy Barnevik? CEOs were once rarely seen and only occasionally heard. Today, that is no longer the case. CEOs have become celebrities. Many are household names. Think of Steve Jobs at Apple, for example.

The high profile CEO may also hold the role of chairman, but it is in his or her role as the dynamic first executive – driving the company forward – that he or she makes headlines. In other words, it is the CEO as action man or woman that we have come to revere, rather than the chairman alter ego as thoughtful leader of the board.

The elevation of the CEO to the status of heroic leader is a relatively recent phenomenon. Its roots can be traced back to the lionization of Lee Iacocca at Chrysler in the 1970s. Iacocca was 54 when he joined the Chrysler Motor Corporation as chairman and CEO in September 1979. During Iacocca's time at Chrysler he executed one of the most impressive turnarounds in automobile history. When he arrived, the Detroit press was full of gloomy headlines such as "Chrysler losses are worst ever." Chrysler was running out of money, and fast. Iacocca took swift remedial action: he eradicated excess inventory; renegotiated contracts with car rental companies Hertz and Avis; recruited a slew of top talent; and made substantial layoffs.

As Iacocca cut costs (he cut his own salary to $1), and the automobile market picked up, Chrysler's flagging fortunes revived. In 1983, Chrysler made a profit of $925 million. Iacocca was feted as the savior of the company – there was even talk of him standing as a US presidential candidate. In 1983, not long after a new stock offering, Iacocca wrote out a historic check for $813,487,500 to clear the balance of the company's debt outstanding on a government loan. Iacocca also collected a bushel of apples from the Mayor of New York who had bet Iacocca that the city would repay its federally guaranteed loans before Chrysler did – the city still owed more than $1 billion.

While Iacocca's fame was well-earned, it marked a sea change in attitudes and expectations. Until the late 1970s, it was widely understood that the chairman ruled the corporate roost. There were – and still are – good reasons for this.

The chairman is the leader of the board and ultimately responsible for what the firm does. The buck stops with the chairman. As the leader of the board, it is to the chairman that shareholders, regulators, employees, and customers look for reassurance that all is as it should be. He or she must be the conscience of the corporation. Even in the United States, technically, the CEO reports to the chairman. Remember, too, the chairman hires or fires the CEO, not the other way round.

But the question of who provides day-to-day leadership in a modern company is a different one. The difficulty lies in figuring out where the role of the CEO ends and that of the chairman begins, and vice versa. At a senior management seminar, held in

New York, for example, one young, talented, and vociferous senior manager of a global insurance company observed: "The CEO runs the show. The top team drive the organization forward." Interestingly, he then went on to add that when the company found itself in difficulty "the chairman got us out of trouble."

Such comments are not uncommon. Often, they confirm that the CEO is in the driving seat while the company appears to be moving in the right direction. But, when it finds itself in trouble or a change of direction is required, it is the chairman, with the support of the board, who seizes the wheel and makes a sharp turn, or hits the brakes. In fact, this is one of the acid tests of a good chairman – the ability to let the executive team, led by the CEO, have their head when things are going to plan; but also to pull in the reins sharply when required. World-class chairman achieve this subtle balancing act. They provide "pivotal" leadership when required.

No wonder then that the chairman can look at times like a passenger in the car. If the CEO is doing a good job, the chairman may appear to be superfluous or simply an expensive figure head. "The chairman just looks after the board," commented another manager. His chairman, he said, was a "nice guy," socially skilled, attending to the affairs of the board, but largely invisible. An invisible chairman is never the ideal – and increasingly rare – but there are times when he or she fulfills the role best by keeping out of the way.

This should not be confused with not paying attention. The chairman should always have his or her eyes on the road ahead and the car's instrumentation. For practical purposes, only the chairman, or a majority of independent directors, offers an effective check on executive power. The chairman is someone who can assume the role of hands on leader when required. A good chairman is the best safeguard against executive dictatorship.

Clearly, some chairmen do not provide alternative leadership. They simply turn up for meetings, enjoy a good lunch, tell war stories, and rubber stamp the CEO's decisions. A few years ago, this was a more common state of affairs. Chairmen were often retired CEOs, who wanted a business interest but preferred a quiet life.

Happily, in recent times, the situation has changed. For this we can thank the unedifying spectacle of a series of high profile executive prosecutions. (Indeed, the real danger is that the role of chairman becomes so onerous that no one will want to take it on.) In the United Kingdom, it is now increasingly rare that the chairman is a retired CEO anticipating a less demanding and less prestigious role. Leading the board professionally and effectively is a role with a huge number of demands and expectations.

Chairman of Anglo American, the gold and diamond mining group, Sir Mark Moody-Stuart is in the front line in the debate about sustainability and relationships between corporations and society. CEOs, he acknowledges, are feted by the media. Their faces adorn magazine covers. Their career moves, opinions, and personal lives are grist to the celebrity mill. Meanwhile, their bosses – the chairmen of the world – take a back seat. Chairmen have the capacity to hire and fire but a tendency to eschew the limelight. This, reflects Moody-Stuart, is as it should be. "It's quite right that they don't get much publicity because it's the CEO's job to be in the front line, not the chairman's."

If you had to create a template for the corporate chairman, Moody-Stuart would be a likely candidate. Born on a sugar plantation in the West Indies, his first taste of education was at Antigua Girl's School. The rest of his career has been more conventional, but distinguished by its peripatetic progress. Moody-Stuart, fluent in Turkish among his other accomplishments, was a natural globalist long before globalization.

Most of Moody-Stuart's career was spent with the oil company Royal Dutch/Shell. Armed with a doctorate in geology from Cambridge University, he worked as an exploration geologist for Shell in the Netherlands, Spain, Oman, Brunei, Australia, Nigeria, Turkey, and Malaysia. He was chairman of Royal Dutch/Shell from 1998 until 2001.

There was, he laughs, no master plan:

> It was more or less step-by-step. I certainly didn't set out
> with some great goal. Having done a doctorate, you're then
> faced with a choice: do you stay in academia or do you go
> into the commercial world? If you believe that science is an
> elegant way of solving problems, then you realize that it
> doesn't matter that the question is asked for financial rea-
> son; the enjoyment comes from cracking the problem. And
> then I widened out from that to other aspects of manage-
> ment, and so on. I was given opportunities, asked to do
> things in many different countries, and presumably someone
> thought I did them reasonably well, so I progressed.

Having left Shell at the age of 60, rather than disappearing off
on his yacht – one of his passions – Moody-Stuart took on
another challenge at Anglo American. He is also on the boards
of Accenture and HSBC, but quickly points out that being chairman of a public company is a big job and he wouldn't contem-
plate taking on another chairmanship. "You have to have an
absolute commitment to that company so that when there's a
problem, it's the number one." In addition, he is involved in an
array of initiatives and causes – everything from chairing the
Global Business Coalition and the G8 Task Force on Renewable
Energy to being president of the Liverpool School of Tropical
Medicine.

Moody-Stuart is a natural chairman. So, what's the job description for the chairman of a large corporation? "It's to lead the
board – the executive and non-executive directors and the chief
executive. The board's role is basically governance, strategy and,
very importantly, the appointment of the chief executive."

The chair leader

So which came first: chairman or CEO? The answer is the chairman. The chairman was and is a central, historical point of reference, dating all the way back to the 18th century. The chairman
was the first distinguished executive to lead the board meeting.

At the time, this was literally a board that people gathered around, often no more than an old door or a large flat slab of wood with two supports at either end. The roles of CEO, managing director, and president all came later. It was the chairman who had to win and keep the confidence of investors, determine the nature of the business enterprise, and hold the managers and employees of the company accountable.

To understand why the role of chairman became so central we need to examine the historical development of boards and the firm. It is also necessary to understand why different philosophies of enterprise and governance developed as they did in different countries. In fact, our research identified nine different governance models around the world, but we will focus on two to illustrate the point: the Anglo-American and the Continental European approaches.

The Anglo-American model gives primacy to shareholders. The shareholders own the firm and the board is charged with acting in their best interests. All other interests – employees, customers, management, society at large, are subservient to shareholders' interests. In effect, the bottom line is, well, the bottom line!

In Continental Europe, however, in countries such as Germany, France, and Sweden, a very different model has developed. Best described as the stakeholder model, it asserts that the board is accountable to not just the owners but to a portfolio of stakeholders that includes workers and the wider community. In Germany, this explains why there is a two-tier board, with worker representation. Under the stakeholder model, the board is charged with managing the firm for the long-term good of all its stakeholders. The bottom line is not the only measure of success.

Clearly, these two traditions are very different – and partly explain the tension that can exist between the European and US operations of the same company. Yet, the historical roots of the firm show that the Anglo-Americans and Europeans started from the same point – the creation of wealth on behalf of the community.

A number of factors caused them to diverge. The introduction of double entry bookkeeping; the use of royal charters to enhance trade and commerce; and the effects of the American Revolution and the later Civil War on banking and finance laws and on social and healthcare provision all played their part in spawning contrasting traditions between America, Britain, and Continental Europe. The different legal systems of Continental Europe to those of Britain and the United States further consolidated the shareholder/stakeholder divide.

While these essentially two different forms of enterprise exist, their differences meet at the role of chairman. The chairman is the focal point of reconciliation of a number of contrasting forces, some historically determined and some as a direct result of corporate action. As business continues to globalize and different systems of governance increasingly come into contact, so it will become more and more important to reconcile these differences.

The unavoidable conclusion is that the chairman is vital to the continued successful performance of the firm and of today's new forms of public agency. To see why, let us rewind once again.

Birth of the firm

The governance determining business and social conduct has an impressive history. Scholars associate Innocent IV, the 13th century Pope, with the creation of the first commercial entities that had limited authority to pursue approved trading initiatives. The forerunner of the modern day firm was created by the Church of Rome with the dual purpose of generating material wealth and redistributing it across the community. Pope Innocent IV held that riches were a threat to salvation. Thus, ownership of resources and the benefiting of the community became intertwined.

Governance can be traced back even further, to the Ancient Greeks and Aristotle. Aristotle encouraged trade and the pursuit of commercial initiatives and, similar to the Church of Rome, warned against personal excess. He emphasized the value of temperance and the need for regulation from a higher and trusted authority. From a need to institutionalize temperance was born a key instrument of organizational administration, the charter, initially approved by the Legislative Assembly of ancient Republican Athens, and later by medieval monarchs in their award of trading rights to towns, municipalities, guilds, universities, and livery and trading enterprises. Similar to the ecclesiastical charter awarded by the Roman Church, the very first "firms," constituted by royal charter, were installed to serve the public good as well as to realize profitable gain for the owners who undertook investment risk. The combination of usury and community became deeply embedded. Today, it is better known as stakeholder governance. The trading entities of towns and monasteries existed as a collective so that assets would be protected against royalist-inclined autocrats.

Communitarianism was challenged by a most unlikely candidate: double entry bookkeeping. Developed as a mechanism of control in order to minimize errors in accounting, the seemingly innocuous practice of double entry bookkeeping had a profound effect on social and business conduct.

One outcome was that private life became separated from that of trade and business. From being an adjunct of everyday life and governed by the same rules, business began to develop its own code of conduct. The firm as we know it today emerged as a separate legal entity. This new organization challenged collective ownership. It also allowed for a life span beyond that of its original owner or operator. Organizations had the potential for longevity. Coupled with the royal privilege to award charter status, the first joint stock companies were formed in England and Scotland to support overseas trade, commerce, and mercantilism. The first recorded charter for the sole purpose of business was issued by England's Henry VII in 1505 to merchant adventurers. What followed were royal charters of considerable significance: the East India Company in 1602; the West India Company in 1604; and the Hudson Bay Company to exploit the vast resources of North America. The joint stock company became the popular vehicle for the creation of wealth for 17th century British, Dutch, and American investors.

Those early, volatile, and high-risk investment entities adopted a makeshift form of governance. In England, Scotland, Ireland,

and the colonies, those tasked with the responsibility of overseeing the company regularly met – albeit in a rough and ready fashion. At the place of meeting, a long board was laid across two sawhorses and the group that assembled around this crude table to discuss their affairs later became known as the *board*. The leader of the group became known as the *chairman* simply because the individual sat on a chair, while the others only had stools made available to them.

In the 18th and 19th centuries, this rudimentary form of enterprise unashamedly exploited the resource riches of the Indias and Americas and, in turn, became the capstone of North American industrial enterprise. With unparalleled growth, concern arose over the unfettered power of the board, its directors, and particularly that of the owner/chairman. Ironically, it was in the land of free enterprise, America, and not in administratively pedantic Britain that the first serious attempts for governance were initiated. The New Jersey legislative, in 1791, authorized its first Secretary of Treasury, Alexander Hamilton, and his Society for Establishing Useful Manufacturers, to allow businesses to produce a spread of goods ranging from the cloth for sails to the leathers for women's shoes and to display necessary standards of quality. Hamilton went one step further and constituted an entity known today as auditors but termed at the time, the Committee of Inspectors. The inspectors, independent of the board of directors, were granted legal access to company documents with the power to review all of the firm's affairs. The inspectors became the protectors of shareholder investment. The emphasis on ownership and the fulfilling of the owners' goals became the basis for the shareholder value focus of governance.

So, to summarize: The Anglo-Americans rely on market forces (what academics term external control mechanisms), which allow for the following:

- access to market determined capital so as to better guarantee liquidity;
- removal of restrictions on voting rights in order to enhance liquidity of capital;

- clear rules for takeovers and mergers;
- transparency of decision making in order to protect shareholders' interests;
- the criminalizing of insider trading so that free market balance is not disturbed by investors exercising privileged information.

The very essence of the Anglo-American governance is the defense of the market and the encouragement of investment.[3] Winning and holding the trust of the investor is prime.[4]

In Continental Europe, however, a different model evolved.

Driven by concern for a broader array of stakeholders (or what academics term internal control mechanisms) and with corporate governance determined by legislation, the critical features of many Continental European boards are as follows:

- a two-tier board structure, consisting of a supervisory board and separately a management board, stipulated by the laws of codetermination. (In certain European countries, the corporation can opt for a single or two-tiered board structure);
- a supervisory board composed of representatives of shareholders, workforce, and other relevant stakeholders, with the prime duty to monitor and supervise full-time management;
- no overlap of membership or function between the two boards, although the supervisory board elects the management board members;
- the influence of the banks on the corporation through their voting rights;
- key investment decisions reached through collaborative bargaining, across an array of stakeholders.

Different models ... same driver

As national economies and multinationals become more entwined, the two boardroom traditions are beginning to move together – if for no other reason than the practical issues of running operations in many countries. The role of the board has broadened.

"Life is changing fast. The board and the chairman in the US not only think about profit but give deep attention to broader responsibilities. Thinking about the position of the firm in the broader community is today's reality," observes James Parkel, a former top executive at IBM and now president of the American Association of Retired Persons (AARP).

A similar opinion is conveyed in Germany. "Shareholder value is no longer the buzz word that it was," reflects Dr Bernd Scheifele, CEO and President of the internationally spread German company, Heidelberg Cement. Dr Scheifele continues:

> Shareholder value was typically related to giving share-based bonus schemes to the management to give them an incentive to create shareholder value, even if only artificially inflated shareholder value. The risk is that the management focus is only short-term oriented and not long-term with a clear focus on product range, market position, costs and the quality of the personnel, which are the drivers for long-term success.

Many people, from Germany to America, now accept that the firm has responsibilities beyond those of simply making money for shareholders. There is growing awareness that multinationals, for example, have a duty of care that extends well beyond the letter of the law to include a moral responsibility to help people in developing nations where they operate, to help the environment, and to help a range of other stakeholders. As this view gains momentum, the role of the chairman as the conciliator and conscience becomes more important.

Given this, it is no surprise that the debate about whether the roles of CEO and chairman should be combined moves to center stage. In the United States, the famous Blue Ribbon committee argues that investing the roles of the CEO and chairman in one individual is the root of unacceptable corporate behavior and challenges whether holding CEOs, presidents, and CFOs to ever greater account is going to minimize further corporate wrongdoing.[5]

Support for that view is growing. Veteran IBMer James Parkel asks: "How can the CEO/chairman monitor himself?"

Sue Meisinger, president and CEO of the Society for Human Resource Management, notes, "that having the separation of the CEO and chair roles allows the CEO to have a valuable sounding board for strategy development."

Both Meisinger and Parkel, now in the not-for-profit sector, support role separation. In similar vein, Harvard Business School's Michael Porter argues that US governance thinking should more resemble that of Germany and Japan. Porter's critique is of short termism, driven by the demands of capital markets. The substantial remuneration of senior US executives, particularly when not accompanied by substantial increases in stock values, adds to Porter's case that insufficient attention to R&D, over concern with personal reward and being driven to please Wall Street, undermines the long-term future of the firm.

Despite these critical voices, American governance is deeply rooted in the psyche of the nation. "It's efficient. Decision making is speedy. Clarity of thinking is present. A strong board with a strong chairman/president/CEO drives outstanding performance and success," says Bernard Rethore, emeritus chairman of the Flowserve Corporation. Rethore's view is that the challenge largely comes from academia and the not-for-profit sector. If the critique of role duality is interpreted simply as noise in the system, then little is likely to change.

School for scandal

While there are reservations in the United States, the distinctive role of the chairman is making a much needed comeback there and elsewhere. The reason is simple: the need for ever better governance.

Over the last two decades the public have been exposed to a barrage of boardroom scandal. The financial engineering of Michael Milken, the cavalier attitude to corporate funds at Tyco, and Robert Maxwell's raiding of his company's own pension arrangements in the United Kingdom, have all had shareholders questioning corporate behavior. Damaging corporate meltdowns have exposed ineffective boards allowing conflicts of interest to continue, permitting perverse executive compensation, and shy-ing away from confronting CEOs who abused their power and destroyed value. The board is accountable, even if board members were unaware of developments in their company.

Value destruction has not just been limited to institutional share-holder funds. Thousands have lost their jobs. Small investors of limited means, often attempting to secure a reasonable income for their retirement, have lost their capital. Old age, for many, due to undesired corporate pursuits, means poverty.

Today, governance demands ever greater transparency. Boards are required to display how they monitor management. Shareholder activism is slowly on the rise. The voices of numerous other stakeholders demand to be heard. Winning the confidence of shareholders, the press, the media, and national politicians requires attention. A rebalancing of power is underway from the CEO to the chairman, where the latter is charged with ensuring the financial and ethical health of the firm.

Let us be clear: ultimately, the person responsible for inattention to corporate wrongdoing is the chairman. The last few years are witness to the fact that so much depends on this one individual, not only to safeguard the corporation but the lives and livelihoods of many.

So, across the world, substantial differences of business practice and governance exist, but with one common thread. The requirement is on the chairman to weave through contrasting demands, respectfully attending to business, societal, and governance demands, while keeping the firm on track.

The loneliest chair

"The chairman is about handling conflicts of interest," reflects Vadim Makhov, the young Russian-born chairman of companies in the United States and Italy. Under Makhov's chairmanship the value of two business acquisitions grew by an estimated 400 percent. Chairmen who provide leadership make a difference – no matter what the governance conditions or the board models. "He, as chairman, supports the CEO and us. He encourages, we act! Through him, as a team, we have achieved outstanding value," says one of Makhov's colleagues.

As with Vadim Makhov, so many more than just the shareholders rely on the chairman's ability to reconcile a spectrum of interests. The chairman sets the platform for a sustainable and long-term future.

But, that is not to say that the job is one of constant pleasure. It can be the loneliest job in the world. Technically, the CEO reports to the chairman. By implication, the CEO discusses problems with and is counseled by the chairman. The chairman has no such luxury. The chairman is held accountable by the board, by the shareholders, and, by implication, by the management. The chairman is alone.

And there is a lot to do. The work spread of the chairman is extensive. The span extends from scrutiny of the financial condition of the organization and detailed assessment of risk to considerations of strategy and competitive advantage, concerns of policy determination, and the grounding of a philosophy that strives for ever greater success and sustainability. Detail, strategy, performance, and company values are among the things that fall under the umbrella of chairmanship.

"The CEO leads the operations and the organization. But the chairman is the guardian – or a better word which has fallen into disuse – the *steward* of the enterprise. The totality comes under his care," says G.K. Kelly O'Dea, chairman of Alliance-HPL Worldwide.

Kelly O'Dea, a rancher, entrepreneur, and developer of people, draws upon a term, now less adopted but which captures the totality of the care and responsibility for the organization, *stewardship*. Stewarding covers concern for the individual to determining the moral nature of the total firm's infrastructure, its contractual obligations and interrelationships in the supply chain, its partnering arrangements and outsourcing agreements. In effect, everything that impacts on the operation and reputation of the organization. The chairman is required to accept broad responsibility, without the benefit of directly accessible levers of control. From *"Why is that family in Ohio not happy with us and our insurance cover?"* to *"How can our values captured in our mission be owned and accepted by our outsourcing partners in India and the Philippines?"* – that is the nature and spread of chairmanship.

The ultimate point of discretion concerning what to do and how to do it lies with the chairman. From the makeshift table of the 18th century, having only a chair to sit on, the chairman of the board has progressed to become pivotal to the success of the firm.

Key points

- The origin of the firm was as a vehicle of wealth creation on behalf of the community.
- Double entry bookkeeping and royal charters helped establish the firm as a commercial vehicle for the benefit of its investors and founded the Anglo-American shareholder-determined organization.
- The American Revolution and Civil War and breaking away from the centralist traditions of European and British monarchists and Parliament positioned courts of law and civil contract as fundamental to American business relations and governance.
- Social and healthcare reform and the legal system of civil code preserved the communitarian (stakeholder) perspective of governance in Continental Europe.
- The two-tier board structure of Germany, partly extending across Continental Europe, requires the chairman and the members of the supervisory board to maintain distance from the affairs of the company, while the chairman of the management board acts as the CEO of the firm.
- Board membership between single tier and two-tier boards varies substantially. Representatives of the workforce,

$\rightarrow$

bankers, other external stakeholders as well as the more business-oriented nonexecutive director, hold positions on the supervisory board. The business-focused non-executive/external director predominates the single tier board.
• The chairman's role is where many organizational and societal tensions are reconciled.

Delineating boundaries

> There's a clear distinction between the role of management and the role of the board. That distinction is critically important because the chief executive needs to know that he's got a clear mandate to manage the business and also understands what accountabilities he has back to the chairman.
>
> Ray Webster, former CEO, easyJet

One of the most interesting aspects of the chairman role is that it means different things to different people. In the course of our research we heard many different points of view. Yet everybody we spoke to agreed on one point: to realize a sustainable future, business performance has to be matched by sound governance. A company must not only act ethically, it must also *be seen* to act ethically. That is as it should be.

If, at times, the need to be seen to act ethically appears to dominate the work of the board, then business has itself to blame – or at least the few bad apples that have eroded public trust. It is an indication of how serious the situation has become that surveys in America suggest that business executives now rank alongside politicians, lawyers, and journalists as the least trustworthy professionals!

The damage is not permanent. Trust can be restored. But it will only be restored if the vast majority of companies conduct themselves in an exemplary manner. It is the responsibility of the world's chairmen to ensure they do.

If the CEO is the heart of the company pumping vibrancy through its very core, the chairman is the soul of the corporation, its conscience, its moral keeper. Only the chairman can provide that leadership. Where the two roles are combined, the CEO/chairman must be the heart and soul of the company. They must be brutally self-critical. They must also have the ability to look over their own shoulder – not an easy feat.

There are signs that this is increasingly recognized, even in the United States. Institutional Shareholder Services (ISS) Inc.'s latest survey of 1433 companies that make up the various Standard & Poor's indexes, including the S&P 500, found that 41 percent had separate chairmen and CEO positions in 2006, up from 37 percent in 2005.[1] Only 13 percent of the chairmen were classified as independent, which means that most of the nonexecutive chairmen were affiliated with the company.

So discipline 1 of the world-class chairman is *determine and delineate the role, contribution, and purpose of management and the board.*

To fulfill the role of corporate conscience, the chairman must be clear where his or her role ends and where that of the CEO begins. This is a difficult boundary to draw. To some extent, the roles have to be fluid – depending on the individual personalities, strengths and weaknesses, and relationship between the chairman and CEO. The fact is that no two chairman-CEO relationships are identical. There is no simple prescription or formula, just some guidelines that offer a framework. Our research identified six critical areas where boundaries must be set:

1. **Governance.** The chairman as the leader of the board is responsible for the governance of the firm. That task cannot be delegated.
2. **The CEO mandate.** The chairman must give the CEO a clear mandate to manage day-to-day operations. At the same time, the chairman is responsible for evaluating CEO performance and succession planning.
3. **Discretionary choice.** The chairman has to make personal choices about their own contribution and how they will interact with the CEO, the executive team and independent directors, including involvement with standing board committees.
4. **Role duality.** The chairman must have a clear position on combining an executive (insider) position with the role of

chairman. They must be clear about their authority for day-to-day actions.

5. **The vision thing.** The chairman and CEO must be clear about who sets and owns the vision.

6. **The board team.** The chairman has to ensure there is the right mix of skills on the board – now and tomorrow. This ensures that roles between directors remain clear and mutually supportive.

The first two points are especially important. To some extent they explain the confusion about who is the leader. To return to our car analogy: it is the chairman who is ultimately responsible for the road worthiness of the vehicle and the safety of all those on board – shareholders, employees, and customers. He or she must ensure that the CEO (the driver) is carrying out the necessary safety checks on the vehicle, that there is enough rubber on the tires, gas in the tank, oil in the engine, and water in the windscreen washers. The chairman must also ensure that the necessary licenses are up-to-date and that the paperwork is in order if they are pulled over.

But – and it is an important but – the CEO must be allowed to operate the throttle and steer the car. The chairman sits in the passenger seat. They are there to stamp on the brakes or grab the wheel if required. The chairman and the board should be consulted on the destination, but they must not interfere while the CEO is driving, and they should leave the actual route to the executive team.

Governance: chairman as soul provider

Positioning the company so that shareholders, customers, employees, and society at large recognize and appreciate outstanding performance is the hallmark of great leadership.

John Berndt, member and former chairman of the Thunderbird Business School board of trustees and also chairman of three for-profit enterprises, argues that good governance creates the freedom to drive performance. In other words, by ensuring the company complies with its regulatory and moral responsibilities, the chairman allows the CEO to drive the business forward. (Anyone who has ever sat on a board facing a potential scandal will know how disruptive it is to the day-to-day running of the business.)

As Berndt points out, good governance is good for everyone: "Sarbanes-Oxley, security exchange commissions, the New York Stock Exchange and Nasdaq have all pushed for greater govern-ance, principally to safeguard the interests of shareholders but also customers, employees and even the supply chain." To John Berndt superior business performance goes hand in hand with the transparent monitoring of shareholders' interests.

"I have some consistent golden rules that I apply when I'm struc-turing my role as chairman which starts with: what is the man-agement philosophy of this company and that of the board going to be?" says Sir John Parker, chairman of National Grid.

In the delicate and shifting balance between performance respon-siveness and governance dictate, John Parker, chairman of the United Kingdom's foremost electricity and gas supply company, talks of philosophy as a guide to determining the role, purpose, and contribution of the board and of the company. He empha-sizes philosophy as the platform for determining ways of working between board and management. Only from that understanding can the two critical roles of chairman and CEO be delineated.

The two counterbalancing demands of safeguarding shareholder assets and the encouragement of a proactive performance cul-ture extend to the not-for-profit arena.

"The role of chairman is to set the whole tone of the organiza-tion. The board has to be very clear about what type of organ-ization it's going to be and what are its priorities," says Helen Nellis, former chairman of the United Kingdom's Bedfordshire Health Authority.

The CEO mandate: what CEOs do

No matter what the organization, clear lines need to be drawn between board and management, chairman and CEO.

Somewhat paradoxically this is even more apparent in US firms that have adopted role duality. The holding of two offices (three when the role of president is included) demands clarity of boundaries. "The chairman/CEO of the US corporation, that one and the same person, has to clearly specify what is chairman and board and what is CEO and professional management. Such is the need for both policy and detail and actively laying that out to the board," says John Berndt.

Who does what, where, and when? Does a universal demarcation of duties distinguish the chairman from the CEO? The emphatic response is that it is up to the individuals to discuss the allocation of duties between them and the reason for such distribution.[2] "You have to spend time thinking that out with your chief executive," says Sir John Parker. Ray Webster and John Berndt, one a CEO and the other a chairman, agree on this point. They advocate going into detail to clarify roles and only then deducing how strategy and policy are to be formed and, in turn, monitored.

Mutual agreement on who does what behooves that the chairman and CEO are of a similar mindset. However, not everyone agrees. "You've got to stand back and let the chief executive get on with it," says Lord Clive Hollick, partner, Kohlberg Kravis Roberts, and chairman of SBS Broadcasting and of the South Bank Centre. He promotes a "boss of the business versus boss of the board" distinction between chairman and CEO. The CEO drives the business.

From a Continental European perspective, Viscount Etienne Davignon, the Belgian vice chairman of Suez-Tractebel, social reformer, former public servant, politician, and one of the founders of the European Union, refers to "co-accountabilities between the chairman and CEO." Whatever tasks are allocated to the two roles, it is how consistently accountabilities are exercised by both that makes the difference.

In contrast, an anonymous Australian chairman confirmed with formidable clarity: "I am the one who sets the vision." Meanwhile, Ernst & Young's Herbert Müller contends: "The CEO is definitely the most powerful guy."

Table 1.1 Chairman and CEO: What do we know? Findings from research[a]

Studies – year	Roles
1965	Dependent on each individual's specialization/preference
1966	Jobs shaped by the expectations of individuals
1977	Chair/CEO roles vary according to accountabilities, company structure, and personality
1984	Chairman is consultant/mentor to CEO
1991	Chair/CEO roles vary according to company structure, personal preferences so that chair can be partner, boss, mentor, consultant, and representative to CEO and organization
2004	Chairman runs the board; requires knowledge of industry; is behind the scenes; is independent, and can take charge but only in a crisis.

Notes:

[a] For further information on research on the roles of chairman and CEO see the following:

- R.C. Hodgson, D.J. Levinson, and A. Zaleznik (1965), *The Executive Role Constellation: An Analysis of Personality and Role Relations in Management*, Boston, MA: Harvard University;

- R. Katz and R.L. Kahn (1966), *The Social Psychology of Organizations*, New York: Wiley;

- C.G. Roe (1977), *The Changing Role of the Chief Executive*, Chalford Hill: Jean Macgregor;

- G. Chitayat (1984), *Report of the Committee on the Financial Aspects of Corporate Governance*, London: Gee;

- R. Stewart (1991), "Chairman and chief executive: an exploration of their relationship," *Journal of Management Studies*, 28(5), pp. 511–527;

- P. Coombes and C.-Y. Wong (2004), "Chairman and CEO: one job or two?" *The McKinsey Quarterly: A New Era in Governance*, 2, pp. 43–47.

American chairmen echo these sentiments. Kelly O'Dea favors role separation and positions the chairman as the driving force: "The chairman is *primus inter pares*. The chairman sets the vision. The CEO is the doing, action man."

In contrast, Bernard Rethore, emeritus chairman of Flowserve, positions the CEO as the focal leader of the company: "The CEO predominates. The CEO drives the company and is the face of the company. The chairman role is more in the background and deals with the board."

Reviewing nearly 50 years of research into the roles of chairman and CEO, a similar, mixed picture emerges (see Table 1.1). No universal agreement has emerged concerning the nature, purpose, activities, and contribution of the chairman and, by implication, the CEO.

This variety of views is the result of a number of factors: discretionary choice; role separation; role duality; ownership of the vision; adopting an internal or external focus; and conduct protocol. By far the most influential is the influence of the people themselves: their orientations, their idiosyncrasies, their view of the business, their vision of a future. Roles and responsibilities are up for grabs. People decide.

The roles of chairman, CEO, board member, and top team executive are not easily codified. Rather, they require their incumbents to determine how positions should be played out.

"At the end of the day, thank god, it has to be the people, how they understand their role and how they operate," reflects Etienne Davignon.

Discretionary choice: shaping leadership

Whether as deeper, innate characteristics or as a result of learned behavior, the outstanding leader draws on a spread of personal contrasts in order to induce extraordinary performance from himself or herself and from others.

But how can any one person be accomplished in all of the attributes of leadership? After 7000 or so texts on leadership written since Hummurapi's codes of conduct in 1800 BC, Babylon, (today's Iraq), the simple answer is no one person can.

Frustrated with the never-ending search for the holy grail of the ideal leader, alternative thinking has focused on one underexamined attribute – choice, or the use of discretion in role. How does a leader use the role in order to make that telling difference? That simple question pulls together the intellect behind competitive analysis and strategy, the pragmatism underlying organizational redesign, and the sensitivity and brashness behind powerful communication.

Discretionary leadership thinking focuses on how the individual faces up to the challenges that have to be overcome and through so doing, how they shape their role. The leader determines the goals and strategy they wish to pursue. They find ways round the hurdles that have to be overcome. They draw on the styles that excite others to act. The situation demands of the leader to consider the qualities and attributes required. The individual adapts to the situation but also molds it to their favor. Their strength lies in the quality of adaptation. Some recognize that past success will not help them in their current role and face the uncomfortable experience of developing new skills while being pressured to meet targets. That is their choice. Others kid themselves that a model of success from the past will be their grade for the future. Others who are more realistic, but unwilling to change, leave.

Leaders have broad discretion to determine their and others' role according to their vision. In so doing, they stamp their authority on the organization and provide structure and clarity for others to do their work. Research shows that the two roles with the greatest discretionary latitude requiring clearly delineated boundaries are those of chairman and CEO.[3]

The chairman/CEO relationship is akin to an hour glass. The funnel can be as tight or as broad as its maker desires (Figure 1.1). The boundary delineating process captures the chairman and CEO's vision for the future and their view of the purpose

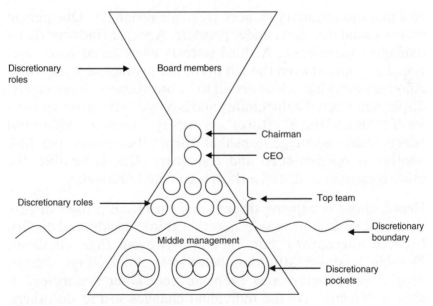

Figure 1.1 The hour glass funnel

and mission of the organization by the very structuring of their roles. Certain chairmen and CEOs set exciting challenges. Others shape their role according to what is familiar. The perspective that delineates the nature and shape of the roles of chairman and CEO molds the other key leadership roles in the organization. The strategy the chairman and CEO agree on determines the number of leadership roles in the organization. An organization that pursues a strategy of cost leadership and that differentiates on price sets clear targets and accountabilities for management. Within a framework of clearly designated goals and activities, the degree of discretion for even senior managers is limited. Although senior by title, the work requires following the prescriptions set by the CEO. Senior managers end up behaving as middle managers.

The converse is also true. A more intricate strategy agreed between the chairman and CEO may require middle managers to make leadership-style choices between providing quality of service and agreeing on discounts for clients while meeting stringent financial targets. In resolving conflicting demands, the middle manager exercises discretion similar to that of a regional/general manager in another organization.

Not that discretionary choices are made rationally. One person makes sound decisions under pressure. Another finds conflict a damaging experience. A third retreats when faced with emotional discomfort even though his or her instinct says stay firm. Another allows himself or herself to be browbeaten. Someone else displays emotional vulnerability and is prone to the psychosomatics of colds and flu. Yet still others display emotional rigidity and rejects ideas and suggestions that disrupt their status quo. Still another is open-minded and responsive. One is flexible, the other is exasperated, and a third is cold and unmoving.

Hence, those occupying discretionary leadership roles display their rational/cognitive side: how they think, decide, and discern between alternatives; but, they also live out their emotions. Nothing is static; attitudes, behaviors, and feelings change; people learn, people regress, people advance. Discretionary leadership is dynamic. As the individual changes so too do others. They take direction from their leader. If for no other reason than their own survival, many predict the mood and emotive state of their boss and adjust accordingly. How many have advised a colleague, *"now is not the time to say anything. Wait till his/her mood is better?"* The leader influences not only by what he or she says and requires, but also by his or her general demeanor.

Being a leader is being visible. It is akin to living in a fish bowl.

The nature of the boundaries between the roles of chairman and CEO and the manner by which they were delineated echoes through the board and through the organization. Board directors and the senior managers in the top team take their lead from the clarity or confusion the two generate.

"I determine the role and tasks of the CEO and of my role as chairman of the board. My management team and board are happy with that. Their concern surfaces when I'm not clear or I swap and change the roles and the boundaries between these roles," says the chairman, president, and CEO of a large US financial services company.

Reality check

- Draw up a list of one good and one bad boss you have known.
- Identify the characteristics of both, highlighting their strengths and weaknesses, attractive features and vulnerabilities.
- How long did it take you to become comfortable with either and with whom could you relate better?
- How long did it take to be wary of the boss you found uncomfortable?
- Study your list and consider the time taken to know how to interact with both?

Now which of those two is more how your subordinates see you?

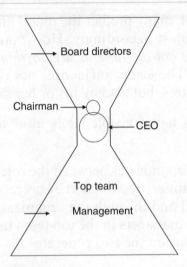

Figure 1.2 US hour glass

Role duality: between schizophrenia and focus

"The British system is fine. The German system is fine. Over here, we Americans feel reluctant to say ours is fine too – but it is. It works for us. I don't see the chairman/CEO/president trio (or duo) changing radically or dramatically," says Bernard Rethore (see Figure 1.2). He highlights three arguments in favor of role duality:

1. **Rank and status.** The individual needs comparable experience and status in order to be heard by his or her peers. Comments Rethore: "A president/CEO may not be heard in a forum of chairmen/CEOs/presidents. Why should he? – the others are ahead in terms of breadth of responsibility!"

Until the individual has experienced running the board and running the business, how can his or her comments be respected? Does a three star general engage with a one star as with other three stars? – No, would be Bernard Rethore's view.

2. **Efficiency and effectiveness of decision making.** In dynamic, fast-moving markets, bureaucracy and an ever greater number of meetings can undermine speed of response. Different individuals naturally come to contrasting conclusions, determined

by personal views and also attending to the particular demands of their role.

"It's not just efficient: it's effective. Having that one person responsible who can clearly overview the situation and lead others," says Rethore. Ultimate decision responsibility in one pair of distinctly capable hands provides that extra edge over the competition.

Rethore has a point. As already mentioned earlier in this chapter, more than half of US companies have one person holding both positions, according to Institutional Shareholder Services (ISS) Inc. And many of these executives are very good in both: think, for example, of Warren Buffett at Berkshire Hathaway Inc. or Jeffrey Immelt at General Electric, or when he had both roles, Bill Gates at Microsoft.

   3. **Culturally and morally embedded.** "It is deep in the American psyche and so too is the moral responsibility that goes with such awesome responsibility," Rethore observes. "The scandals in the press and media are so un-representative of reality."

The argument here is that moral capacity accompanies the holding of senior office. Many top US executives we spoke to talked about moral responsibility. The message is that leading a company is not about exercising control for its own sake but about taking broad responsibility for both the organization and community. Our study supports Bernard Rethore's view that extensive responsibility is accompanied by an acute sense of moral consciousness. Doing the right thing and being seen to so do is not as strongly expressed by the top directors from other nationalities as from Americans.

However, moral sensibility (or the lack of it) is not the concern with role duality. The fact that the same individual drives the management and leads the board has the unfortunate effect of inhibiting challenge and discussion. The inherent weakness is that it limits the discussion because there is only one point of view where there might be two or even three different points of view. Similarly, when something goes wrong there is only one moral compass to detect it.

Role separation

Additional to Rethore's three points is a fourth issue under role demarcation and that is whether a chairman is an executive chairman (an insider) or a nonexecutive chairman (an outsider). What sort of chairman does a company need?

Maurice Newman, the steward of corporate governance for Australia as chairman of the Australian Securities Exchange, interprets the role of executive chairman as comparable to the US practice of role duality. "An executive chairman is where you have the two roles combined, so that the chief executive and the chairman are two persons in one," says Newman.

Others argue that the two roles of chairman and CEO become muddied when a company appoints an executive chair. Says Andrew MacDougall, president of Spencer Stuart Canada, an executive search and corporate governance consultant: "I have yet to see the definition of an executive chairman role that answers the question of who is doing what job."[4]

Don Argus, chairman of BHP Billiton, does not see a problem. "Look, if I do my job properly, I should be able to stand up and articulate the strategy of the company very clearly because I'm closer to the non-executives and they rely on me," he says. His only after thought is, "the CEO gets his authority from the board."

Some give the notion of being nonexecutive short shrift. "I think non-executive is an abuse of English. I don't know what it means. If you have an obligation under the Company's Act ... you have an obligation as chairman. ... I'm talking about being a part-time chairman of a significant complex institution," observes Lord Dennis Stevenson, one of the world's most experienced and eminent corporate chairmen. "I am incapable of being called chairman of an organization without feeling responsible for it. What that involves in practice, first and foremost, is your relationship with your chief executive."

Maurice Newman, Don Argus, and Dennis Stevenson, in offering contrasting interpretations of the role of chairman, draw attention to the following questions;

- Is the responsibility of the chairman to principally chair board meetings?
- How much time does/should the chairman spend on the affairs of the company?
- Does/should the chairman act as the leader of the board and/ or seek broader influence and responsibility?

To further understand these questions consider the role of chairmen in Australia. Here, it has been traditionally a nonexecutive post (see Figure 1.3). However, more due to geographic isolation, the search for top executive talent in Australia's high performing companies, extends abroad, particularly the United States and the United Kingdom. This creates issues of its own. After five years of working abroad, Americans, especially have to either return home or adopt the nationality of the country in which they reside; or pay US taxes on all of their assets, worldwide, as well as local country taxes. Not surprisingly, the vast majority of Americans return home. Many other expatriates do likewise. In these circumstances, who attends to the balance, stability, and long-term future of the company? The chairman does. In Australia, more for the major corporations, some express that there is little alternative other than for the chairman to be executive.

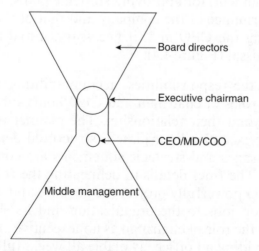

Figure 1.3 The Australian hour glass

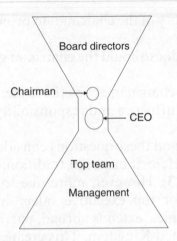

Figure 1.4   The UK hour glass

The British emphasis, in contrast, is on nonexecutive chairmen. In practice, this means working for the company on a part-time basis. Observes easyJet chairman, Sir Colin Chandler: "The chairman provides balance, and in order to show who is in charge, it may not be necessary to have an office in the company."

Chandler, as chairman of easyJet, emphasizes the now common UK practice, that the CEO runs the business. The chairman leads the board and assumes responsibility for governance, for policy development, for approving strategic plans, for monitoring the performance of the company and that of the CEO, and for supporting the CEO and, if necessary, initiating the individual's dismissal (Figure 1.4).

Establishing the responsibilities, accountabilities, and boundaries for the roles of chairman and CEO holds substantial significance beyond their relationship. The manner in which the funnel of the executive hour glass is structured determines the way key messages and strategic statements are communicated and trusted. The finer details in delineating the roles of chairman and CEO powerfully project the purpose and contribution of the two top jobs to the organization and its shareholders. Constituting the role of chairman as nonexecutive and part time but then providing an office, available all week, fully resourced with IT and administrative support, including secretary, contradicts the part-time nonexecutive status. People quickly begin to ask why the chairman, as a part timer, needs these resources. Is the chairman such a strong personality that he/she gets their way? If the chairman is so strong, who really drives the business? Can what the CEO says be trusted if his/her authority may be undermined?

Visions, dreams, and strategies[5]

Shaping the funnel of the hour glass not only delineates boundaries but also identifies who acts as the heart and soul of the organization, pushing forward the strategy and vision.

In the United Kingdom, the CEO typically drives the business forward and is, in that sense, more internally focused. The chairman attends to board concerns and broader issues of risk, reputation, and networking and therefore adopts a more external perspective.

"The chairman is responsible for overseeing governance and ensuring that the chief executive delivers the business plan," says Ray Webster, former CEO of easyJet. Sir Colin Chandler, chairman of easyJet agrees: "Proposals for strategy come from the management teams. I, as chairman, and the board consider and contribute to them."

Moving a further step back from strategy, you encounter the thorny issue of vision. Who owns the vision?

"I think that the vision, that noble goal, needs to be clear and easily understood. If you don't know where the organization is going, if you don't know what the vision is, then you aren't going anywhere," says Sandy Bruce-Lockhart, leader of the UK's Kent County Council. "The role of the chief executive is implementing the vision as set out by the chairman."

Others emphasize the CEO as determining and driving forward the vision, requiring the chairman and board to ratify and support it. Sue Meisinger, President and CEO of the Society for Human Resource Management, emphasizes, "that the CEO plays a critical role in helping the board to articulate a vision, ensuring that the necessary research and options are developed and provided for consideration by the Board." This is how the chairs she's worked with have operated.

Common to US not-for-profit enterprises is the fact that the CEO is not chairman of the board. Sue Meisinger, as President and CEO, in openly supporting role separation, is clear on who determines and drives the vision. However, clarity concerning who owns the vision needs to be accompanied by an equal clarity on what is the vision.

The purpose of a vision for the future is to enable and inspire; to have those in the organization (and in the supply chain) achieve more than they would otherwise have done. Equally, an inspiring vision affects those external. They too become driven and their expectations are raised.

Whatever the vision, most important is that others in and external to the organization, believe it. It is vital that the chairman, CEO, top management, and board are, and are seen to be, in harmony over the vision.

Determining and pursuing the vision is demanding not only because of the intellectual challenge involved but also because of the emotions and opinions that the process of envisioning encourages to surface. In one sense, during the process of visioning nothing new emerges. What people feel should be done, why and to what purpose, has been known for some time. These sentiments have lain dormant and occasionally have caused discomfort. All that changes. Visioning the future is an invitation to participate not only in the life to come but also about reconsidering the life that has been. Through a self-determined purge, previous disaffection is put aside, leaving people free to reposition themselves and the organization.

To not establish clarity and a shared view of the future between the chairman and CEO encourages self-interested idiosyncrasy to supersede shared rationality. The one who shouts loudest may win, not because their thinking and crystal ball is better but simply because of strength of character.

"If only those two could establish a way of working, especially now that we are re-organizing," one independent director of a global pharmaceutical company lamented of her CEO and chairman:

> Both big egos; both brilliant but not when together. They do not have to like each other but acknowledge their different strengths, which we so desperately need, and then clearly and openly establish who does what. We could have a winning vision. Instead we are muddling through, and on certain days even less than that."

Reluctant to be identified, the independent director highlights how not establishing a clear boundary and way of working between the chairman and CEO, particularly when restructuring and revisioning, can have disastrous effects. Two personalities exposed to each other with no governance agreement between them expose the organization to unwelcome politics. When the chairman and CEO do not establish workable boundaries, division is the result.

In such situations no single long-term direction is clear. Contrasting visions for the future are championed by different individuals, each with their own logic and each portraying that *mine is best*. Energy is spent on dissension rather than promoting the business and fighting off competitors. The resulting contradictions are costly as they lead to duplication of effort. Splits of vision can even become an endemic part of the culture. Pulling in different directions becomes a norm. Bypassing formal channels of communication and accountability becomes an undesired but accepted practice. Any attempt by the member of the top team to approach the chairman "to talk things through," without the CEO's knowledge, can be as damaging to trust and transparency as the chairman wanting to find out about the organization and organizing site visits without the CEO's knowledge or agreement.

"Some of the executive directors came to me complaining about both the chairman and chief executive and others. It was sort of like juggling balls," comments Derek Bonham, former chairman of Imperial Tobacco and others, describing an earlier and disruptive situation of divided vision (but not at Imperial Tobacco).

Strained relationships and divided loyalties lead to resentment and distraction from taking charge. Dissonance in the chairman-CEO relationship positions the enemy as within.

Organizational lack of direction breeds a brand of disabling empowerment. Through the need to survive, each individual gains the confidence to push his or her own agenda, increasing the chance of contradiction and further conflict. For middle managers, observing senior management dissention and the lack of unity and clear direction from the chairman and CEO, emotional resignation sets in. Why bother? Who is listening? Why challenge when others who have done so in the past faced retribution?

If this cascading dysfunctional behavior is to stop, the chairman and CEO must decide their rules of engagement. They do not have to agree with each other or even like each other. But they need to create and communicate a vision. They need to agree on the following:

- Who determines the vision?
- Who drives forward the vision?
- Who vets the vision?
- How to jointly set an example for the rest of the organization?

The board team: mix and match

"What does the board pack look like?" asks Jeremy Pope, chairman of the £700 million UK business, Milklink.

Clarity of role and contribution between the chairman and CEO precedes the next consideration for the chairman: the role, contribution, and boundaries of the board.

The Australian Institute of Company Directors identifies three prime functions of a board: to appoint management; oversee managements' performance; and enable management to improve performance.[6]

Few would disagree. Viscount Davignon formerly of Suez-Tractebel and currently of CMB adds a fourth: "Clear delegation to management and clear accountability of the board to management."

In fact, various bodies, commissions, and authors have identified a number of functions for boards, namely to do the following:

- monitor the financial well-being of the firm;
- monitor the performance of management;
- appoint the CEO; dismiss the CEO; monitor and appraise the CEO's performance;
- monitor, review, and approve senior management appointments;
- monitor management succession;
- monitor the development of management;
- set policy and practice for management remuneration;
- approve individual senior management contracts;
- monitor, review, and approve business strategy, business plans, and goals;
- monitor and review risk by setting down risk assessment protocols;
- specifically examine the level of risk exposure resulting from particular investments, contracts; or transactions;
- guard the reputation of the firm;
- approve critical statements for the press, media, or other stakeholders;
- review and approve statements, reports, and other documents to shareholders or other critical stakeholders.

The effective exercise of such functions requires attention to three considerations: board composition, board functioning, and respecting boundaries.

1. **Board composition.** It is up to the chairman to identify and gain agreement of the skills required by the board. The involvement of the CEO in this debate is particularly critical.

"I see the board bringing a group of skills that complement the staff," says Kate Davies, CEO of the Notting Hill Housing Trust. Even as a public service organization providing for the accommodation needs of a broad spectrum of Londoners, Kate Davies emphasizes the complementarity of skills between board and professional management. "Board members need to stay at a high level otherwise they get bogged down and are not useful," she says.

Board members attending a limited number of meetings have to earn their credibility through recognizing the nature of their contribution. The Notting Hill Housing Trust board includes members who understand about building homes, the organization's main activity, as well as others with HR experience, IT experience, and experiences as customers.

Sir Colin Chandler extends functionality to a broader set of board skills, for the nonexecutive directors:

> We've got the CEO of one of Holland's biggest cable companies which gives us a European dimension. Another director brings creativity through her TV background and others come from the hotel and travel industry, from financial services, and from academia. We have too the unrivalled entrepreneurial skills of our founder. So I think it's the mixture.

CEOs and chairmen universally concur that it is the chairman's role to determine the skill mix of the board. "A good chairman works diligently to make sure the board has the right mix of skills," says Michael Chaney, chairman of the National Australia Bank.

In similar vein, Sir John Parker takes diligence beyond the realm of individual discretion to the level of designing a structured framework. The framework should incorporate the breadth of skills needed, capture the current skill disposition, and emphasize skill shortages. The benchmark for the framework is the business plan of the organization. "This comes down again to a disciplined framework. Everybody should know their role (and by implication, each other's) when they are meeting," he explains.

Through adopting the Sir John Parker line, not only does each director know what is required of them but through establishing a skill set framework, each knows how to also draw out relevant contributions from the other.

The search for the perfect skills mix is never ending and can lead to some unusual selections. In 2006, the BBC newsreader, Anna Ford, became an independent director of Sainsbury's, the large UK food retailer.[7] Explaining the appointment, Sainsbury chairman Phillip Hampton said that Anna Ford would:

> take particular interest in corporate social responsibility. The board is strong on financial analysis but we are not strong on other things. ... There are a lot of fundamental issues in the business under the heading... Sunday trading, food labelling, selling alcohol to minors... sustainable fish stocks. We felt a businessman would have less feel for this.

Whatever the motivation of the Sainsbury board, at least the appointment criteria for Anna Ford were clear.

In our research, involving all board members in the search for new directors was emphasized. "You go out to headhunting firms and ask them to get a list and then you run the list by your existing directors. Yes, I know that person (or not)! So word of mouth and reputation is still important, as it ought to be," says Michael Chaney.

The recruitment process is especially important for a relatively new breed of board appointees: the lead independent director (LID, United States) and the senior independent director (SID, United Kingdom).

"The lead independent director intervenes, in fact, must intervene in circumstances of crisis and transition," says Bernard Rethore. This is especially true in the United States where the CEO and chairman roles are typically combined. Our research suggests LIDs are important counterbalances to join chairmen/CEOs. By default, the LID becomes chairman of the board, albeit temporarily (Figure 1.5). To do so, the LID must already have won the support and respect of the board. Business experience and a capability and wisdom befitting a statesman are the factors that cluster the board around the LID.

The LID is half in the funnel of the hour glass and half not. High performing LIDs make their presences felt not in terms of

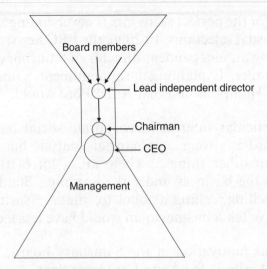

Figure 1.5 The extended hour glass: the US chair/CEO and LID relationship

intervention (except in crises) but in practically improving the functioning of the board.

A US chairman/CEO/president of an international manufacturing company observes:

> Together with the lead independent director, we set the agenda for the board. We discuss those issues that need to be addressed and thus discover problems before they arise. We have a good working partnership but with challenge built in. Having a lead independent director is most useful. From what I see, many do not know how to use them.

The accomplished LID does not suddenly appear at the time of crisis. The involvement in board affairs is continuous. Of value is feedback to the chairman concerning operational matters, on how the board meeting was received by other board members, and the polling of views on matters of strategic and project importance.

The service of counsel extends to the period of transition, the appointment of a new CEO. Embedding the individual into the organization is invaluable. Offering guidance and supportive comment maturing the CEO to also become chairman, is equally appreciated.

As Bernard Rethore says:

> Our lead independent director holds meetings with the board directors after the formal board meeting, when professional management are not required and that includes me (as the chairman/CEO). I also leave the room. The LID gathers views, offers counsel, smoothes over key concerns. We then sit together and discuss that. The benefit for me is simply un-measurable.

The funnel of the hour glass is extended. The LID has potentially a foot in three camps: the board, the chair/CEO role, and the management team. Yet, as Bernard Rethore suggests, the accomplished LID rarely migrates from the role of board member. He or she offers independent counsel, canvasses views, and works together with the chairman/CEO to prepare for meetings ahead. Outstanding LIDs are rarely center stage and yet continuously make their presence felt.

Elsewhere, senior independent directors have a more vaguely defined role than their American counterparts. In the United Kingdom, for example, the counterbalance to the out of control CEO already exists in the form of the nonexecutive chairman. By implication, the British SID is the counterbalance to the counterbalance. Although SIDs provide similar operational contributions to LIDs – drafting agendas, gauging opinion, offering feedback to the chairman, and ensuring adequate information – disquiet about clarity of the role is far greater.

Certain SIDs contend that lack of role clarity is more down to the individual and their inability and unwillingness to communicate with the chairman and CEO when other board directors are unable to do so. "Independence is a state of mind and possibly a state of pocket book as well. I've known people who I thought were independent but when push came to shove, you're not quite sure," notes Derek Bonham.

The SID is the point of last resort but, this time, on behalf of shareholders (Figure 1.6). Says experienced chairman, Tony Alexander:

> Where the fault line is beginning to emerge and people are getting worried, then your next point of call should be the senior independent director – we're worried! We've talked to your chairman. We've talked to your CEO and we don't buy what we are being told. What's really going on?

For Tony Alexander, the SID is the shareholders' route into the board and the company, when all else has failed. This view is not universal. Some express concern that the SID is required to do what other board members should have done. Why then have a board? Shareholder and other stakeholder disquiet is the responsibility of all board members. As one SID commented: "My presence ensures that the other board members are not discomforted."

Whether acting as a safety net to minimize a crisis, or to smooth over executive transition, determining the role and contribution of the LID and SID falls squarely on the shoulders of the chairman. On this all agree.

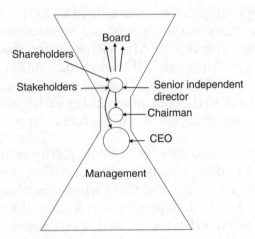

Figure 1.6   The extended hour glass: the UK chair/CEO and SID relationship

2. **Board functioning.** "Make sure the board is involved, that there is a detailed agenda, people are regularly informed and that the key issues are given a full airing," advises Lord Clive Hollick in summary of the chairman's role in ensuring a smooth running board. He refers to six protocols chairmen should apply. According to him each chairman should determine the following:

- the agenda;
- the quality of information to board members;
- the timelines of information given to the board;
- the length of board meetings;
- the number of board meetings;
- the nature and purpose of board meetings.

To this Lord Burns adds a seventh: do all six but *together* with the board directors. "People debate, so that they understand what it is to have a high degree of predictability on behalf of the board, – in order to respond to various types of situations and prevent misunderstandings of challenges," says Terry Burns, chairman of Abbey National, chairman to Marks & Spencer, and Welsh Water, among others. The involvement of all board members encourages ownership of the process of discussion and the resulting conclusion.

All of this seems basic, but inadequate attention to board functioning is commonly the root of larger problems.

One form of dysfunctionality is not receiving the right data at the right time. A second and more challenging dysfunctionality to overcome is that of data saturation. "At one time, I was sent 140 pages of data covering every operating unit worldwide and I mean 140 pages of figures, narrow typed. Just because I started demanding some financials," recalls Rosalind Gilmore a former independent director at Zurich Financial Services.

It is up to the chairman to determine the nature, volume, and quality of data presented to the board. Only when information is appropriately formatted can board members fulfill their monitoring and audit duties.

A third form of recurring dysfunctionality is for board directors to not appreciate the totality of issues and concerns facing the company. It is the chairman's responsibility to act as the interpreter of strategy. "I regard the main role of the chairman as being to ensure that the board has a shared understanding of the strategy of the company," says Terry Burns.

The CEO's contribution to the strategic debate is to enhance clarity through detail. "Make your subject easier to understand for the non-executives. It is easy to run rings around them in detail, local knowledge, local language. You have to remember independent directors are not in the business, they come in and out of it," advises Gareth Davis, CEO of Imperial Tobacco.

Ultimately, the chairman guides the contribution of the CEO. Equally, the frequency, length, and type of board meetings are dependent on the chairman's view of need and requirement. Commonly reported are monthly board meetings accompanied by away forums for discussion of strategy and possibly additional meetings for specialist inputs. More frequent meetings are a response to crisis.

Derek Bonham was chairman of Marconi during its most difficult period. "At various times, we had to go through weekly board meetings... we did them in the evenings to try to get the majority of people there," he recalls.

A minority of chairmen hold quarterly board meetings. With only four meetings per year, little opportunity exists for board directors to become more knowledgeable about the organization.

3. **Respecting boundaries.** The CEO of an international telecommunications company complained to the authors of this book thus:

> We brought in one of these governance gurus and spent a day on "high performing boards." We all agreed, ask for detail but do not get involved in daily operational detail. Management can just get on with the job. What happened? Next day, the board wanted the daily minutiae and started telling management what to do. The chairman is the worst of all!

Shortly after, the CEO resigned to be followed by another who, in turn, left within the year. The better senior and middle managers also left. The fractures in the structure became publicly evident within two years. Share price dropped. The company was acquired. The existing board and some of the management were retired.

Involvement and interference are universal problems. "In Turkey this problem is endemic and difficult to solve. Second and sometimes third generation family shareholders, board members are interfering with the professionals. Let the professionals run the company," says Ishak Alaton, chairman and founder of Alarko Holdings in Turkey.

Practices that survive three generations are difficult to break. However, change is needed, especially if Turkey is to survive in the modern world and particularly if Turkey is to become a full member of the European Union. "About 15 years ago, I wrote an article, 'How to make yourself unnecessary; how to make yourself obsolete'. It's still relevant today," says Ishak Alaton.

The bottom line is clear: Despite resistance and sensitivity, if current ways of board working are considered ineffective, it is up to the chairman to redetermine boundaries. Once boundaries have been agreed and clarity exists, not respecting reporting relationships and agreed ways of working only causes harm.

Key points

- The chairman, together with the CEO, determines the boundaries between the roles of chairman and CEO, between board and management.
- Determining meaningful boundaries requires consideration of the nature of the company, of the strategy being pursued, and from that understanding the allocation of responsibilities between chairman and CEO.
- Attention to the chairman-CEO relationship is critical to the effective functioning of the board and the organization.

$\rightarrow$

- The context and the personalities involved profoundly influence board functioning and board contribution.
- Despite differences of role and responsibility between chairman and CEO across the world, consideration of who owns and drives the vision of the company significantly affects the nature and quality of relationship between the two individuals and between the board and the top team.
- To hold and pursue differences of vision, or to not agree on who determines and vets the vision, results in chaos and continuous dissension.
- Consideration of the challenges facing the organization and how key responsibilities are divided between chairman and CEO, according to who is best suited to meet these challenges, clarifies the more internal or external focus for the two roles.
- Respecting a conduct protocol between chairman and CEO and between board and management ensures that boundaries are maintained.
- The chairman, together with the CEO, determines the skill profile of the board.
- The chairman, together with the CEO, determines the process and procedures for board succession.
- The chairman determines the level of involvement, the range of responsibilities, and the contribution of LIDs and SIDs.
- The chairman determines the type and quality of information presented to board members as well as the purpose, structure, frequency, and length of board meetings.

Sense making

> You need a strong empathy and a very powerful desire
> to identify with the goals and mission of the organiza-
> tion that you have been invited to chair.
>
> Lord Tom Sawyer

Working in the same organization is no guarantee that common agreement exists on the challenges facing the organization or on how to move forward. Tension, mistrust, and pulling in different directions are an everyday reality. Ask a board or a group of senior managers about the market challenges and strains confronting the organization and you will hear a variety of views and opinions. In reality, the vision of the future does not need to be nailed down to the smallest detail. Events dictate that the best-paid plans can unravel. There are no watertight five-year plans. This is as it should be. No leader has a monopoly on wisdom. No board has all the answers. No chairman is omniscient.

But, there has to be some degree of shared understanding of the world out there today and in the future. There has to be what Sir Colin Chandler calls, "a common understanding of what the business is about."

Providing a shared sense of what the organization stands for and where the organization would like to be is the second key discipline of world-class chairmen. They help people in the organization make sense of the present and the future so that they and the organization can maximize their performance now and in to the future.

This discipline is about helping others to make sense of past and present processes and events so that a shared understanding of the strategy, vision, and mission of the enterprise emerges for both the board and management. Shared understanding acts as a primary platform for action; it provides the confidence that the leadership of the organization are of one mind. Visibly evident shared commitment at the levels of the board and top team, in turn, bonds together everyone else in the organization.

This begins with some key business questions:

- What is the competitive advantage of the firm?
- Do customers recognize the value this firm provides?
- Is it the reality that most customers can barely tell the difference between one company's services and the next except for those at the very top of the value chain?
- Is price the only real differentiator from the customer's point of view?
- What do shareholders expect in terms of return on their investment?
- Is greater value to be gained from keeping the enterprise together or separating out the assets for sale?

Would the people in your organization answer these questions on the same foundation of knowledge and aspiration? Word-for-word, learned by rote answers are not what is needed. People need to sing from the same hymn sheet and at the very least know that such a sheet is available (hopefully from the chairman's office).

Sense making for chairmen has eight demanding attributes:

1. Start with passion.
2. Acknowledge diversity.
3. Attend to the chemistry factor.
4. Delineate strategic responsibilities.
5. Canvass reality.
6. Review progress.
7. Encourage feedback.
8. Limit damage.

Start with passion

Sense making begins with passion. Displaying a passion for the mission is exciting and infectious. Others voluntarily push themselves to succeed through performing beyond expectations.

We have learned a great deal about passion from the former trade union leader, social reformer, and politician, Tom Sawyer. Now Lord Sawyer, he insightfully redesigned the UK's Labour Party providing a strong platform for Tony Blair's reforms. As comfortable with sorting out labor disputes as with working through top management wrangles, Tom has chaired the boards of public service agencies and private sector enterprises alike. He believes there is one fundamental factor which has to be in place to achieve compatibility of thinking at board and top team level: passion for the mission. People have to believe. Passion begins at the top.

Of course, the reverse also applies. Where there is no passion, it is unlikely that the chairman will be able to transmit belief to those around him or her. Tom Sawyer recalls one appointment which did not work out, and that was because, he explains, "I did not feel some level of passion about what the organization stood for."

Desire, coupled with a logic that rationally justifies the next steps to be taken, provides for a common platform of understanding and the will to act. "Look carefully and calmly and say I really do think that it is very worthwhile doing. I think I can add value to the organization," concludes Tom Sawyer. Tom recalls the chief executive of Marriot Hotels telling an audience that there was only one way for them to find out if he was doing his job properly – when they went to their hotel bedrooms was the toilet paper neatly turned up? "The chief executive is in New York and wants to know the woman in Hong Kong who cleans the bedroom knows what do to. The principle is good," says Tom Sawyer. "As a chairman, I ask myself what's the toilet roll test in this business?"

Acknowledge diversity

Global organizations are melting pots of emotion, argument, dispute, and disagreement. In order to not be swallowed up with strife and tension, the chairman must acknowledge the diversity of views that exist within the top team. He or she should then work towards reaching a meaningful conclusion on vision and strategy as a management team.

Indeed, being able to harness diversity is increasingly vital.[1] Look around. The western world is reaching, and in many sectors has reached a point of market maturity. In order to be more competitive, most organizations have invested in adopting the latest tools and techniques from sales or marketing to IT. Yet, for the consumer, differences of quality of service and product across a range of companies are minimal.

Diversity can be a differentiator and yet, in all likelihood, is also likely to expose more disparity of views. The question is how much? Is that difference more of an irritant or a real problem?

Our global research highlights that Irish and foreign companies located in the Republic of Ireland report high levels of dissonance concerning a vision for the future at top team level (Table 2.1). Also, and surprisingly, Hong Kong Chinese-based corporations, with a tradition of hierarchical family ownership structures, report that 42 percent of their top managers hold deep differences of view concerning future direction and vision. And, in the public sector, 56 percent of senior public servants in the Australian Public Service report deeply divided views concerning the future shape, structure, and direction of their service. Such divisions are the chairman's agenda.

However, the process of envisioning a future is not tidy. Seeing ahead, foreseeing events, avoiding crises, preparing for change, and in turn positioning the organization is the rational side of visioning. It is the sense-making side. Visioning also involves

Table 2.1 Differences of vision at top team level[a]

Sweden	NHS Top Team	NHS Board	Japan	Finland	United Kingdom	Austria
20	20	21	23	25	30	31

Germany	China	France	United States	Spain	Hong Kong	Ireland	APS
32	33	39	39	40	42	48	56

Note: NHS – National Health Service (UK).
APS – Australian Public Service.

Source: [a] For further information on differences of view of vision, see A. Kakabadse and N. Kakabadse (1999), *Essence of Leadership*, chapter 8, p. 296. London: International Thomson.

Tom Sawyer's passions, inviting challenge and involvement from others and emerging with a shared belief on the direction to pursue. Shared belief releases a creative energy, allowing for a redesign of critical corporate functions so that the vision can be kept on track while the organization is responsive to external change. Driving the enterprise forward requires the passions of Tom to initiate and maintain momentum, but it must also be rational. Visioning is both revolutionary in its intent and goals, as it is evolutionary in its step-by-step logical progression. Both are required, or damage will occur.

Studying chemistry

What is chemistry? In the context of the chairman's role, it is all about how individuals in the boardroom react with one another. Understanding chemistry is a sixth sense, a nonrational but, nevertheless, powerful guide about what is happening now and likely to happen in the future. The evidence says, do not worry; progress is on track and in keeping with the plan. But doubt creeps in, a doubt that is not paranoia but more a questioning as yet unsubstantiated by data. Without evidence, challenge may be difficult, and in the eyes of colleagues, even destructive. Yet, to wait for sufficient data to emerge could be too late. Rationally, all makes sense. Instinctively, something is not right.

The ultimate challenge to the process of sense making occurs when the case for action, on the surface, is proven but the individual harbors doubt. Yes, sense making is dependent on models, facts, and numbers but also on years of experience, particularly concerning relationships. The hard and the soft have to co-exist.

The chemistry between us provides for nonrational glue that binds a shared sense of purpose and direction. Chemistry is a shared interpretation of events and information, a personal affinity: the exhilaration that arises between two people. Chemistry is also the comfort of seeing the world in similar ways.

One of our interviewees was Major General Steve Rippe, executive vice president of the Protestant Episcopal Cathedral Foundation in Washington, DC. He said of his relationship with his

Bishop: "I'm very close to the Bishop. We both hold a philosophy of grass roots, decentralize, get close to the people. We have
supported each other throughout this change process. It has
been a memorable experience and very fulfilling."

Pat Molloy, former chairman of one of the largest companies in
Ireland, observed:

> There should be good chemistry between the two [chairman
> and CEO] based on mutual respect. The chief executive
> should feel free to consult with the chairman anytime, at any
> hour, day or night. The chairman should be available to him.
> Respect comes from the chairman having something to bring
> to the party, having something to add. For the chief execu-
> tive, he knows he will get the chairman's support at the board
> meeting and not have the rug pulled from under him.
> Different levels of understanding of the business exist on the
> board and with management. Having said that, when they
> sit around the board table, execs and non execs should really
> see themselves as members of the board as opposed to hav-
> ing one hat or another. They come from different places but,
> with the right kind of chemistry, they will be respected and
> challenged and proceed as one.

Chemistry is built on a similar interpretation of events, personal
affinity and group membership. The group in this case is the
board. Having a seat on the board, irrespective of executive or
nonexecutive status, requires wholeheartedly accepting the
responsibility of membership of the board. Shared interpretation, close affinity, and board membership are the three elements of a close and binding chemistry.

Depth of chemistry influences the quality of interaction between
chairman and CEO, between board colleagues, and between the
board and the top team. Particularly in roles of senior leadership, where the discretion to determine the shape and nature of
the role is extensive, each person displays his or her deep-seated
sentiments. Two individuals may agree with each other on the
strategy to pursue, but their inability to respect each other makes
the relationship and the strategy they have agreed to unworkable. Two others may not fully agree on the strategy or even on
relevant details concerning the daily management of the business

but feel comfortable to challenge each other without fear of damaging the relationship.

Such deep sentiments are commonly termed values – what each person truly values. Certain individuals predominantly value outcomes. They are driven by tangible results. Whether they like or dislike others is totally immaterial – friend or no friend, can you do the job? Others more value conduct, ways of speaking, and doing. Certain people may consider it rude to swear, and on hearing a term of abuse, irrespective of how it was intended, find it difficult to listen and respect the other party's point of view. Thus, two individuals theoretically suited to work together as chairman and CEO because they share similar experiences or industry knowledge may find it in practice difficult to tolerate each other's presence. The manner by which they address each other causes tension, irrespective of the topic of conversation.

The mix and match of values determines each person's approach to task and goal completion as well as their leadership style. People carry their values on the sleeve. The value predispositions of the person are evident to others. How they think and feel strongly determines the manner of response of others. Of course, the skill is to be conscious of one's own value orientation and how that influences others. Such sensitivity and awareness is deeply appreciated and profoundly and positively shapes the morale and motivation of those around.

The three sides to the chemistry factor – similarity of interpretation of events, congruence of the more deeply held values, and deep feelings of responsibility and loyalty to the board – ignite the most electric of relationships, when in parallel. Particularly, between the chairman and CEO, when the chemistry factor works, so many describe the experience as enthralling and memorable. Others around are equally infected by a buzz that exponentially increases the work tempo.

Delineate strategic responsibilities

Passion and chemistry are the right lab conditions for strategy. But who takes the lead? The more common practice in the

United Kingdom, and even with the more dominant profile of the Australian chairman, is that the CEO, together with his or her team, formulates strategy and then surrenders the strategy to the chairman for initial scrutiny.

"It is for the chairman to ask the really hard questions of the CEO on behalf of his board," says Don Argus, chairman of BHP Billiton. "We get the board to write things that they believe should and should not happen. We have breakout sessions. It's got to be a working board. The days of boards just sitting there like a sponge and absorbing, are gone."

What follows is a distillation and refinement through discussion between chairman and CEO. Some have described it as an untidy process which stretches the relationship, but, if respectfully conducted, it provides for a further strengthening between the two. Once accomplished, the board can be engaged.

Australian chairmen behave in a more dominant way in the strategy distillation process than their UK counterparts. The more proactive Australian chairman requires a more proactive board. UK boards more reflect the position adopted by the chairman in the strategy formulation/distillation process. "I regard the main role of the chairman as being to ensure that the board has a shared understanding of the strategy of the company," reflects Terry Burns.

Irrespective of the variance of styles, when the chemistry factor works, the discussions are enlightening and exhilarating. Accomplished strategy formulation, its distillation, and interpretation of strategy for the board depend on the quality of relationship between the chairman and CEO.

"If there's not trust, then there is no basis for negotiation. There has to be a mutual trust and a clear understanding of what each does," considers John Phillips, chairman of Australia's Foreign Investment Review Board.

No matter what the cultural differences concerning the passivity or proactivity, establishing a clear and agreed position on the strategy development continuum between the chairman and CEO precedes fruitful discussion of present and future events

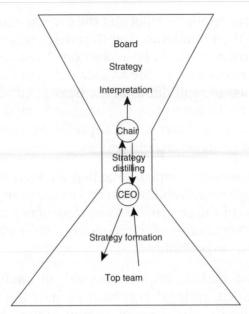

Figure 2.1   Hour glass: strategic dissection

and developments (Figure 2.1). As John Phillips emphasizes, trust, together with clear responsibilities, enriches strategic sense making at the level of the board and top team.

In the United States where CEO and chairman roles are commonly combined, clarifying the chairman/CEO's contribution to strategic sense making requires careful consideration.

Reflecting on the role of his chairman, the Bishop of Washington, Major General Steve Rippe, recalls:

> He provided clear analysis of why we could not continue as we were; why responsibility had to be passed down to the schools and Cathedral. He cleared that with me, his number two, and then with us, the management team and then presented that as policy to the board. Not only did he make sense but how he went about it and made clear what was management's responsibility and what was the board's, brought us all together.

The issue facing the newly appointed Bishop was financial viability, despite the Foundation's not-for-profit status. The Bishop requested Steve Rippe to report on the current and future challenges facing the Foundation and to provide recommendations on how to proceed. The report positioned the responsibilities and goals of management side-by-side with the policy risk and reputational assessment duties of the board. Although unusual for a not-for-profit enterprise to pursue role duality, nevertheless, the Bishop, as chairman/CEO/president, clearly specified delineation of strategic responsibilities.

John Phillips concurs, emphasizing that the logic for the allocation of strategic responsibilities is not just the prerogative of the CEO, but also of the chairman. "The chairman needs to have a very good understanding of the economy within which the company operates," says Phillips.

Strategic sense making requires breadth of analysis accompanied by detailed, rational argument on how to proceed, supported by a specific allocation of responsibilities. Yes, take into account the chemistry factor and be sensitive to people but, above all else, be rationally clear. As Bernard Rethore says:

> Board members want to hear your business understanding. Appreciated is the fact that they have direct access to the guy who runs the business. They want your business wisdom and not your ego. When ego pops up, they just push it back down. All can be forgiven except for one fact, that you do not know how to take the organization forward.

Irrespective of role separation or role duality, clarity of strategic thinking and tactical application is demanded and evident when not forthcoming. Bernard Rethore continues: "I have seen boards lose faith in their chairman/CEO when woolliness enters the debate."

Canvass reality

Our research clearly highlights that one-third of the world's top teams admit to visioning tensions. To make matters worse, two-thirds of senior management are uncomfortable about discussing and facing up to their concerns (see Discipline 4: Influencing outcomes, Table 4.1). Lack of clarity prevails.

This is particularly clear when they discuss something as basic as sales and marketing. The chairman, too, is a salesman. This was brought home when we read of Dick Boer's appointment as CEO of Albert Heijn, a key subsidiary of the Dutch retailer, Ahold.[2] Shareholder impatience with the Ahold group was abated with Boer's rapid success in, "slashing prices and boosting sales." The next stage was to "develop recommendations to accelerate plans to drive and fund identical sales growth across Ahold's global retail network." The Ahold board was reported to have agreed a three-year recovery plan with each geographic area having its own goals to achieve. In addition, the group has to emerge with "a 5 percent operating margin goal." The road to recovery is clear to all – it is a sales strategy.

The terms sales and marketing induce a wide-ranging response. Research across seven separate sectors and 5,000 managers concludes that different organizations attribute different meanings to sales and marketing.[3] Three sectors provide an example of the degree of variance (see Table 2.2).

No common pattern emerges by what is meant by sales and marketing. Our study emphasizes that in the well-run company, the CEO and the management team held a clear and shared view concerning the value, contribution, and structure for the functions of sales and marketing. However, the majority find it difficult, as a senior management team, to discern a clear difference between sales and marketing. As a consequence, the functions of sales and marketing overlap. Marketing takes on sales responsibilities and vice versa. A reluctance to examine and redesign the structure for fear of disrupting delicately balanced management relationships also emerges. Senior management know the sales and marketing organizations are inefficient, poorly structured, and have overlapping activities. Few dare to say anything.

No such concerns are there at Goldman Sachs, whose chief executive, Henry Poulson, Jr., proclaims: "We are very much a client driven firm. We are very good advisors. We have client relationships that are second to none."[4] Under Poulson, the firm recorded an annual profit of US$5.63 billion in 2005. The board and management at Goldman's are of one mind. The firm is well differentiated, makes best use of its sales and marketing, and offers high value to shareholders and customers.

Table 2.2 Top managers on sales and marketing

	Sales	Marketing
Manufacturing	• Customer relations • Customer needs • Trained sales force • Service • Pricing • Technical support • After sales service	• Customer service • Price/cost • After sales service • Advertising/image • Market research • Quality • Product development • Technical expertise
Transportation	• Communicating with customers • Tailoring service package to clients • Cost effectiveness • Pricing • Customer-oriented staff • Customer care for repeat business • Product demonstration • Delivery efficiency • Quality	• Brand awareness • Global market understanding • Client service • Market network • Public relations • Identifying/meeting client needs • Tailoring to customer requirements • Ensuring for repeat business • Quality
Financial	• Gaining client confidence • Pricing • Product offering • Breaking down customer resistance • Expertise of staff • Quality of product • Professionalism • Awareness of competitor offerings • Understanding/meeting client needs	• Client contact • Understanding/meeting client needs • Targeting clients • Professionalism of advice • Branding/advertising • Strong sales team • R & D • Human resource planning • Pricing

Unable to agree on the fundamental parameters of sales and marketing, how can companies meaningfully trade? Not that managers hold differences of view in order to be difficult. Difference reflects how each manager experiences sales, marketing, and competitive advantage in their locality. Why should a strategy devised at the corporate center hold similar weight in a region or country? Contrasts of local and regional context, such as consumer habits, discretionary consumer spend, and varying laws and codes of governance, require consideration of the value and relevance of corporate center-determined strategies. It is not the chairman's role to intervene in what is, essentially, a challenge for management to sort out how they interface and operate. However, it is the chairman's prerogative to canvass reality of whether the strategic plan will work.

Thus, in canvassing reality, is the chairman

- aware of strategic tensions between the members of the top management team?
- conscious of the spread of views of vision and strategy amongst the management?
- informed as to whether the CEO commands the respect of the top team?
- convinced the CEO is doing the best job possible?

Has the chairman

- probed the CEO about how effective is his/her process strategy formulation?
- informed the board of how well (or not) the process of strategy formulation is proceeding?
- explored with the board whether the strategy, the reality of strategy formulation, on the performance of the CEO requires scrutiny?

The degree to which the chairman has unearthed strategic reality determines both the quality of strategic plan and the board's faith in the management of the firm.

Says Tom Sawyer: "If you feel there are certain weaknesses down the line, or in certain parts of the organization, then, as chairman, you've got to spend some time on those things. It is always important to discuss these with the chief executive and his team and the board directors."

Review progress

Convincing the board of the coherence of the strategic plan is one consideration. Keeping to the plan some way into its execution is another. The imperative to meet short-term targets is inescapable. Keeping to target becomes increasingly difficult when the strategy considered in Corporate Center, Chicago, is out of step with market requirements in Russia and Eastern Europe. The chairman's appreciation of the pressures senior managers face in keeping to the plan determines what questions are asked of the CEO:

- In the cold light of day, was the strategic plan, as originally conceived, too ambitious?
- Has the tension between what the CEO terms as stretching and what senior management consider as impossible proven the CEO to be right or not?

The chairman has to consider when to intervene. For joint CEOs and chairmen this is a potentially schizophrenic experience. "It is up to me to determine when I am CEO and when I am chairman, I give deep consideration to how I, as chairman of the board, report progress on plans and strategy when I refer to myself as CEO," says a US chairman/president/CEO of an international IT company. Certain chairmen consider intervention only when absolutely necessary. Yes, by all means, when a crisis looms. Others affirm that better still is to bypass crisis.

To protect the integrity of the two roles it is worth establishing under what conditions the chairman would become involved. In the pursuit of the strategic plan, the boundaries between the chairman and CEO are likely to be revisited. It is worth reaching understanding of how boundaries are to be repositioned in dynamic circumstances. The sense shared by the board and the management cannot be allowed to be undermined by a confusion that should have been foreseen.

Encourage feedback

Irrespective of national difference, role duality, or role separation, the translation of strategy into practice is the prerogative of the CEO. The subdivision of labor lies with the CEO. The CEO promotes the vision down the organization. On the invitation of the CEO, the chairman contributes to the promotion of the message. Yet, in the CEO's domain of strategy application, the chairman should pose one question: To what extent has the CEO checked out and challenged the progress being made?

Has the CEO encouraged feedback, particularly of the difficult to raise but genuinely held road blocks to making the strategy work? Courting positive and negative feedback not only surfaces concerns before they become problems but also stimulates senior management to think more broadly. An additional benefit to inviting feedback is that the commitment to the strategy is visibly enhanced if those tasked with making the vision work can be easily accessed. Whether the chairman and CEO are equally involved in feedback exercises is a question of personal leadership style and philosophy. What responsibilities are attributed to the chairman and CEO in establishing a culture of feedback is the outcome of discussion on priorities and protocol.

"The board wants to know when they are talking to the chairman or the CEO when we address the challenging and stretching subject of vision. Know how to present yourself and for which audience," advises a well-known US chairman/CEO.

Whatever feedback channels are initiated, whether focus groups, team meetings, business breakfasts, or social gatherings, the positive effect is that teams and whole units are glued together. Encouraging feedback nurtures partnership. Straightforward conversation without fear of reprisal encourages the cultural change that follows implementation of the strategic plan. Display of unity from the chairman and CEO cultivates a common language for the organization, which, in turn, cements the experience of change in the present and establishes a foundation of future well-being.

Sense damaging

All the steps to attain a shared making of sense of challenges and events and the direction to take in the future have been taken. Still something is missing. Despite all efforts, the personal affinity between the chairman and CEO, or between board members, remains low. Different interpretations of the same events continue to the point of becoming a habit. Colleagues walk into the boardroom with their loyalties remaining outside. Duty to the board is not foremost. Definitely, something is wrong.

It is time to take stock. Sense vetting, or as one chairman described it, "the fluffy audit," is now necessary.

It is the chairman's responsibility to ascertain the depth of the problem. Are the tensions inhibiting the emergence of shared common sense, more due to little affinity, little common ground concerning rational analysis and interpretation of events, or little loyalty?

Ironically, under tension the reasons for poor common understanding become clearer. Through attentiveness to understanding what is happening, why is there little meeting of minds on how best to handle the situation emerging? From investing time in the relationship to sponsoring a particular program of development, irritants to reaching common appreciation can slowly be sidelined.

Describing his experience of trying to improve his relationship with the CEO of the organization where he was chairman, Tom Sawyer says: "I actually liked the bloke. I had a very open relationship with him. He always said the right things to me. He would say 'I know what I can do. How do you think I can improve? I did everything I could.' He was a good man and I believed he needed every opportunity to prove himself." Despite the lack of common understanding, at least with Tom Sawyer and the CEO there was a personal warmth.

The converse is shared business understanding but little or no affinity. The lead independent director of one global company provided us with this appraisal of her CEO and chairman:

> Both are brilliant. Both share the same vision but there is no warmth. I believe both try hard to keep their dislike hidden. In that sense, both are professional. But there is no excitement at meetings. No zing. Meetings are sterile. We (board directors) never quite know how to contribute. To challenge one may give advantage to the other. I hope one of the two leaves but that seems unlikely. We could be like this for years, always showing potential but never quite pulling it off.

Unwilling to be identified or even to hold discussion on the company's premises, the independent director described a state of continuous tension between the chairman and CEO. The basics of stewardship were accomplished but little more. More challenging conversations became rarer. To raise the subject of relationships undermining bad performance could offend the CEO, who, as an individual, was an admirable performer. To not do so could be interpreted as lack of loyalty to the chairman and the board. Board meetings all too quickly attended to the lowest, but acceptable, common denominator.

With no shared mind-set and low affiliation the result is paralysis. All involved know what is wrong, and even know what to do, but find themselves unable to act. At this stage it is time for the LID or the SID to act. But, to act too soon could damage the reputation of the organization with unwelcome attention and scandal continuing long after the removal of either the chairman or the CEO. Alternatively, to delay taking action seriously undermines realizing the ambitions of the organization.

Too often, little is done, negativities are absorbed and denied, and the tension continues. Why? Well, for a number of reasons.

Ego

First there is *ego*. Ego is the predilection of the other but not of me! Irrespective of nationality, culture, religion, or gender, when damaging tensions prevail in the boardroom, the word ego is commonly used to describe the other party, who is seen to be the problem. The CEO of an international financial services company confided that his chairman

> was full of himself and nasty with it. Everyone else gets it wrong and he is right, or at least that is the impression I and others have. He is just impossible to talk to. Whenever he asks a question, he does not want an answer. What he wants is confirmation – "tell me I am right!"

Again, unwilling to be identified, as much due to a strong sense of loyalty to the chairman, the board and the organization, the CEO in question continued at length about his frustrations with his chairman. The chairman, undoubtedly talented, is even better networked. Even within his circle of contacts and friends, independent comment confirms his arrogance that many describe as an overblown ego. The CEO, himself a strong character, at least recognized his own need to dominate. As we spoke, the CEO was seriously contemplating resigning. He asserted:

> What will happen is that he will again hire someone like me, a strong and powerful CEO, and the whole cycle will repeat itself. One good think to come out of all this. I know just how much of an ego I have. It is good to take charge but not be so self centered. I will try to do something about this.

Divide and divide again

As long as I get my way! The humility to put emotions to one side for the greater good is not an approach to influence that some have adopted. Some rightly argue that to do so accentuates the problem. Yet, instead of confronting current circumstances, some, whether chairman, CEO, or board member, enter into further "political dissension." The aim is to isolate the other side and divide and divide further the board in order to isolate the so-called problem person.

Listen to this independent director describing his chairman:

> He is a strong personality, but also divisive. Nothing is taken head on. If you agree with him, you know. If you do not, you find out later through some sort of machinations behind your back. He talks to the other board directors privately and you find yourself isolated with the decision already having been made.

Unwilling to break rank and tarnish the reputation of the organization, the director declined to be named in his description of his chairman. The organization was well networked into government. The chairman was championed and supported by government. Reality, however, was a deeply divided board. Unable to appropriately respond to challenge, the chairman inhibited debate and entered into the politics of one-to-one, behind-the-scene understandings with board members. Acclaimed as an intelligent and farseeing person, the chairman's capacity to lead the board was diluted through a myriad of unproductive maneuvers. For the CEO, strategy was nonexistent. The organization tumbled from one tactical solution to another. It was not long before the CEO resigned. Today, few suitable applicants are making themselves available as contenders for the position. The chairman continues to be in place. With the person's reputation in the outside world intact, the board expects similar divisive practice once the new incumbent is in place.

Sullen silence

For how long can dysfunctional relationships and situations continue? Well, from one day to over 50 years. Just like a marriage that should amicably have ended years ago, the relationship continues with each party losing out on realizing better opportunities in life. What is worse, they become accustomed to dysfunctionality. Sullen silence reigns. What should be said is not, and so the situation continues.

"It was a bad time. The relationship between the two (chairman and CEO) was hugely divisive," one director observed. "Argue one point would cause the other to take the counter point of view. Most sat in silence. We virtually ended voting but not discussing or challenging."

One prominent independent director recalled the period before a well-known company suffered a collapse of share value. The description was of a weak chairman, an arrogant CEO, and an additional, forceful director. That trio cowered the board into sullen silence. No challenge was taken as agreement. All on the board knew that silence meant submission and being taken down a road none wished to travel. The independent director recalls thus:

> Even when challenge arose, the executive director brought in advisors to the board meeting to show how we were wrong. The chairman just let him do it. What's worse, these consultants

did not leave. They remained for the rest of the board meeting. After a while no one said anything.

Even unwilling to identify the role title of the executive director for fear of attracting a law suit, the independent director described how he and his colleagues fell into silence after being "proven to be wrong."

The sullen silence continued for a good 40 months before the "true health" of the organization became public. The independent director, like other colleagues on that board, denied irresponsibility and wrongdoing. Technically they were not fully informed. The true financial health of the organization was not fully disclosed to them. The question remains as to the extent they denied their suspicions.

"You've got a board of directors who have some deal going on. The financier says, "okay, it's clean!" The auditor comes in and says, "okay, it's clean!" Well they both said the same thing so it's okay. And then it's not," says Tony Alexander.

When questioned, numerous board directors and senior managers considered themselves as able to withstand continued dysfunctionality. Tony Alexander, chairman, and board member to numerous boards, counters that view. "You're very vulnerable to those situations," he says and our study confirms Tony Alexander's observation. Until challenged, many consider themselves strong enough to withstand strained relationships. Sullen silence is an uncomfortable, undiscussed, but common phenomenon. How many of us have sat at a meeting, or in the boardroom or at home, knowing what needs to be said but saying nothing? And how many have continued day after day, night after night, still not raising that initial concern?

Breaking the cycle

"I've experienced companies where there has not been a good relationship between the CEO and chairman. There was an obvious fault line between the two. It's the chairman's job to put that right," says Tony Alexander.

The way out of dysfunctional boardroom relationships is for the chairman first to recognize the source of the tension. Consider who offers more to the organization, the chairman or the CEO. Resign or fire the CEO, is what Tony Alexander recommends: "A good chairman knows how to do that. There aren't many good chairmen around."

Recall the CEO working with Tom Sawyer we mentioned earlier. After sending the CEO on a business school course and one-to-one mentoring, Tom satisfied himself that he and the CEO were unable to see the world in a similar fashion and he was not meeting performance requirements. Tom Sawyer then took the painful step of removing the CEO. "Eventually, I had to get rid of the chief executive because he never fulfilled that obligation to me or the board," he recalls. "You've got to have a strong board because of the adversity and difficulties you face. Build up the board but I also learned not to get too close."

In addition to concluding who (chairman, CEO, board member, or even executive director) provides the greater value, Tom Sawyer suggests deliberately strengthening the board to face up to stretching discomforts.

To not act encourages idiosyncrasy to supersede rationality. The biggest "bully" wins, not because their thinking and crystal ball is better than others but simply because they overwhelm others.

Knowing when to depart is a wisdom in its own right. So, too, is knowing when to stay. In the end, it comes down to forcing the issue rather than allowing it to fester. The most important thing is to act.

But whatever mechanism is adopted, resign, sack the CEO, change the mission of the organization, or change the composition of either the board or the top team or both, the cycle of sullen conspiracy simply needs to be broken. One chairman brought the top team together and used strategic planning to provide for new thinking. Through confrontation, he induced a break with past behaviors.

Another approach is to relentlessly charm and influence.

Nick Johnson is CEO of Bexley Council in the United Kingdom. Nick describes his challenge of working with a self-obsessed chairman: "We don't know how to cope with this man. He's unbearable! He's so awful. He's so pompous!" I said,

> you know how you have got at home a lilo, you know one of those airbeds where you put it on the floor and you push your foot on it, – there he is in your room – pump, pump, pump and he'll go away happy. I need this idiot to decide something. So how do I do that, I've got to work with this personality.

In his role of CEO, having to deal with elected politicians, when all else has been tried and failed, Nick Johnson recommends flattery. Swallow hard and bolster the self-image of the chairman. The individual will sooner or later leave the post. Irrespective of the irritation experienced, the community requires service to be provided. The elderly, the frail, and the disadvantaged should not be affected by internal, personality-dominated battles. Sense of responsibility for others overcomes self-indignation. Nick Johnson says:

> I am very motivated by ethical issues. I believe very passionately about rights. It's difficult because the personal values that motivate the chairman may be out of line with the personal values that motivate the manager. I do make sure to reach out to those people who've traditionally not had opportunities. That's very important to me personally.

Of course, flattery has its limits; it can also prolong the status quo.

Making sense

A shared way of seeing the world is the essence of making sense together as a board. Tony Alexander terms the phenomena as "compatibility of thought lines." Having taken the necessary steps to realize compatibility, or to minimize further damage,

John Phillips of Australia's Foreign Investment Review Board suggests the outcome can be put to two tests:

Test 1: Can the chairman go into a meeting without silence and know how far he can go with the board because he knows them, he's worked with his board, and understands them?

Test 2: Does the board itself have the confidence that the chairman will never step beyond what the board will accept ... In other words, the chairman won't be running back and checking everything ... he will get it right 99 percent of the time?

In essence the questions are: Can the chairman truly represent the board? Does the board openly and meaningfully trust that the chairman has got his story right? If the answer to both is yes, then there is every chance that the board has achieved shared sense making.

Key points

- It is the chairman's responsibility to foster an openness of relationships to reach a shared understanding about the nature and purpose of the organization, the internal and external challenges, and the direction to take in the future.
- Sponsoring a positive chemistry requires the chairman to attend to the three elements of sense making: personal affinity, similarity of interpretation of events, and loyalty and duty to the board.
- Attentiveness to the chemistry between the chairman and CEO is particularly important as that relationship powerfully influences interactions on the board, on the top team, and between the board and the top team.
- Making sense together as a board and top team does not happen by chance. Continuous attention to building relationships and reaching common understanding and purpose are required.

$\rightarrow$

- Steps to achieving shared sense making involve acknowledging the diversity of views and values that exist at board and top team level; being conscious of how the chemistries between top players affect shared ways of thinking; appropriately delineating strategic responsibilities between chairman and CEO; canvassing reality in terms of how strategy is being implemented in terms of marketing, sales, and competitive advantage; displaying conviction and belief in the strategic plan; and reviewing progress through encouraging feedback.
- When all necessary steps to achieve compatibility have been taken and still deep differences of view are evident, it is time to vet why the chairman, CEO, other board and top team members hold different realities on how and why to move forward.
- To break the cycle of negativity and dysfunctionality, consideration has to be given to deciding who is best suited to leave, changing the players on the board and top team.
- Two key tests: Can the chairman truly represent the board? Does the board meaningfully exhibit its trust in the chairman to represent them?

Interrogating the argument

Nothing is personal and should not be taken as such.
Many have the intellect, but not the personal stamina
for the heat of discussion!

Vadim Makhov,
Chairman, Severstal North America

Discipline 3 is about asking questions, providing an alternative view, being a skeptical voice when all are in agreement. It is the chairman's job to create a culture of constructive dialogue, to interrogate the argument, to provide intellectual due diligence, and to push and question in search of the best solution.

A primary function of a board is to monitor. Irrespective of whether the board more proactively determines strategy and policy, as is often the case in Australia, or examines initiatives shaped by management, the case submitted requires scrutiny. The argument and supporting details need interrogation – or penetrative analysis, as one chairman put it. It is the chairman's job to ensure that executive proposals receive that scrutiny.

Aside from ensuring the success of the proposal, reducing risk, and safeguarding the reputation of the organization, one additional and powerful benefit from interrogating the argument is commitment. A robust management putting forward a well-prepared case that is analyzed in a systematic and logical manner not only strengthens the case but also encourages greater commitment from those involved. Working together to improve the proposals put before the board enables all concerned to identify with the outcome as well as allowing recognition of each other's strengths and contribution. Well-positioned logic and constructive criticism strengthen relationships rather than damage them.

It is the chairman's job to ensure that submissions to the board are insightfully examined, while enhancing relationships between board members and that between the board and management.

In his mid-thirties, Vadim Makhov is chairman and has been chairman of companies as well as head of strategy for the Severstal Group, the Russian steel giant. He speaks perfect Russian, English, and French and is adept at dealing with individuals and groups. Friendly, warm, and always polite, Makhov exudes a confidence that encourages board members and management to speak their mind. "I use myself as the example," Makhov says. "I always question but never hurt. I explore but never put anyone down. As chairman of the board, my job is to create a context and a set of practices that allows members of the board to get to the heart of the case but emerge as friends."

No one is saying this is an easy task. Far from it. It is actually one of the hardest skills for a chairman to master. It is also one of the areas where the chairman requires skills different from that of the CEO. To some extent, CEOs can rely on bombast to interrogate a case. The effective chairman uses a more subtle, nuanced style. The job of the CEO requires them to ask the right questions of their reports. The job of the chairman is to create the environment and context in which the right questions are asked by others. Simply put, a chairman who behaves as grand inquisitor is likely to be isolated from the executive team and would be unable to provide a sounding board to test ideas.

Encouraging criticism requires resilience and robustness. Resilience is needed to respond positively to comment, even if critical, and recognize that the contribution is worthwhile. Such resilience is essential in order to gain from the debate. This requires the chairman to build and maintain robust relationships. Trust is essential to engender transparency and open understanding between the chairman and CEO and between board and management. Interrogating the argument without resilience and robustness turns positive contribution into a defensive nightmare. Certainly one fact is clear. Examination of any proposal requires the challenging of assumptions and the critique of the logic and consistency of the argument presented.

In the heat of discussion, standing back and recognizing the benefits to be gained from stretching analysis not only requires a sharp and logical mind but also a personal quality to not take offence and instinctively assume that critique is a cover for personally directed criticism.

Our interviews with chairmen identified five steps to positive interrogation of the case before the board:

1. **Break down the argument into workable components**. In breaking down the argument, the chairman coaches the management to emphasize the relevance, alignment, quality of supporting evidence, and logical sequencing of the argument.
2. **Position the argument**. The chairman determines the quality of discussion in verbalizing the argument. He or she fosters dialogue and discussion. Dialogue encourages in-depth, uninhibited exploration, whereas debate induces a win/lose situation, the taking of sides, being for and against, so that the most powerful presence in the room carries the case, irrespective of whether that is the best argument.
3. **Manage expectations**. Through cleverly positioning the argument the board and the management team are better prepared. One should remember, too, that no board likes surprises.
4. **Have a full and frank discussion**. Exactly what full and frank means will depend on the individual situation. A board made up of directors who know each other well may be more or less polite in how they discuss the issues. However, all boards must discuss the issues present. The form of discussion depends on the psychological contract between chairman and CEO. This contract varies and is negotiated over time by the parties concerned. It is an implicit understanding about speaking openly. The aim is to have all members of the board fully involved in the discussion, while being aware of the need to ensure that they all have a contribution to make.
5. **Rework the argument**. Sound discussion is provided if expectations have been appropriately positioned. Once the interrogation has run its course and further work is necessary from the management team, practical steps to reworking the argument and winning final approval add a final sense of completion.

Breaking down the argument

In-depth discourse and examination require that the argument be broken down into its component parts. Ask the following questions:

- What is the *relevance* of the proposition to the organization and its strategy and policies?
- How well is the case *aligned* with other initiatives being pursued?
- What is the *commitment* of management to the initiative?
- What quality of *evidence* supports the case?
- How well *sequenced* is the argument justifying the case?

Relevance

Aclan Acar, experienced banker, top manager, and now board member, currently Doğus Otomotiv CEO, described that when as CEO of Turkey's Ottoman Bank he took steps to improve the risk management capability of the organization. A proposal was submitted, together with external providers, to develop the risk management systems of Ottoman Bank. "We needed risk management qualities on the board," recalls Aclan Acar. "We got a proposal from them. They designed a risk management system for the bank, which covered market risk, operational risk, credit risk and so on. We were far ahead of what government did."

The quality of the submission was evident. The ensuing scrutiny of the proposal, and its acceptance and implementation, led to the appointment of an additional board member whose prime responsibility was risk management and assessment.

Thus, in breaking down the proposal, the first question is, what is the value to the organization? Before a detailed examination of the case proceeds, the value-to-whom consideration requires scrutiny. A good idea that contributes little to the enhancement of the organization is not worthy of further board attention.

"Should we really be in their markets? Should we really diversify in this way? But that's strategic debate. That's where you really want the non executives to engage the executives. At the end of the day, you are there to create value," reflects Sir John Parker.

Alignment

This is how *Fortune* described Mark Hurd, the then newly appointed CEO of HP (Hewlett Packard) following the dismissal of Carly Fiorina as CEO:

> Hurd gets jazzed by diving into sales numbers – he jokes about "interrogating the data" until it confesses. Fiorina loved the limelight; Hurd did not want to be on the cover of this magazine. Fiorina owned Davos, the annual teach-in for "Plutocrats" in the Swiss Alps; Hurd skipped this year's session citing "customer commitments." Fiorina was always on message; Hurd is sales optimization in a suit.[1]

The article emphasized the differences of vision and approach between Mark Hurd and Carly Fiorina. Particularly visible is the alignment Hurd created between market opportunities and the company's strengths. "Hurd boils down HP's opportunities to three market trends that neatly match the company's three main units... no matter how you dress up his views, he is simply trying to leverage the things HP is already good at," the story continues. "It's as if a new CEO of Procter and Gamble were to demand – what else can we do here with toothpaste and diapers?"

Hurd dismantled the centralized selling group and reversed the Fiorina structure of combined printers and PCs. Despite layoffs, a reduction in R&D spending, the introduction of certain global promotion schemes, and a freezing of pension benefits, management and the work force seem to be behind Hurd. Having also brought in new management talent, the results of his endeavors are a 29 percent increase in profits (profit of $5.6 billion on a sales turnover of $91 billion) and a 65 percent increase in share price.[2]

Fundamental to the revitalized HP is alignment – alignment between vision and strategy, alignment between strategy and action. Mark Hurd has created a sales-driven organization that has increased profitability and improved share price. Under Hurd, technology application has received similar treatment. The number of computer centers have been reduced from 85 to 3 and the information technology (IT) projects owned by line management reduced from 1200 to 500.[3]

Alignment provides a two fold advantage, the reduction of complexity and greater clarity by clearly displaying the links between initiatives. Clearly positioned relevance and alignment already has the board on side. The value proposition is clear. From now on, interrogation focuses more on detail.

Evidence

"The support from the chairs at SHRM has been tremendous, but it's always been built on the notion of 'trust but verify.' We provide data-rich information to the board on the organization's performance," says Sue Meisinger.

Factual detail is the fuel of constructive interrogation. In similar vein, Mark Hurd's "interrogate the data until it confesses," emphasizes the imperative for explicit evidence. Evidence captures the merit of the case. Evidence draws out the counterarguments, distinguishing assertion from well-balanced argument. A clear display of point and counterpoint assists the board in reaching a shared and balanced view.

Sequencing

Accompanying attention to detail is sequencing.

"We have open discussion and challenge. It helps the debate but also helps the clarity of thinking behind the debate. The case has to be well constructed from every angle," says Pat Molloy, former chairman of CRH in Ireland and chairman, Enterprise, Ireland.

The quality of the evidence may be impeccable. But, the positioning of evidence requires equal attention. Sequence the argument, clearly displaying the step-by-step logic of the case. Even if flaws exist, they too should be made transparent. Weaknesses exist in virtually every case. Highlight these as well as the logic of the proposal; then support for the proposition put to the board is likely to be more forthcoming. Appreciation of the totality of the argument is likely to guarantee commitment to proceed.

Commitment

"I always ask, are you committed to this project and have you the team really behind you?" says David Clarke chairman of Macquarie Bank. No matter how well thought through is the case put before the board, the commitment to turn ideas into action needs to be evident. Feeling the desire to drive the proposition through to success reassures the board.

From the management side, Peter Cummings, chief executive, Corporate, Bank of Scotland agrees:

> We go round each other and analyse every detail. We need to get our story straight but also we need to be sure that everyone is of the same mind. Nothing goes forward until every little detail is thrashed out and we all state we are fully behind this one. We attend board meetings and we go forward as one voice and it shows.

Peter emphasizes the final phrase, *"and it shows."*

Visible signs of commitment are as fundamental as quality of argument. Michael Chaney, chairman of the National Australia Bank, told us of his emphasis on "creating an open atmosphere in the boardroom where directors feel welcome to speak their mind ... Directors feel if they raise an issue, they are able to keep raising it and pursuing it until they are satisfied with answers."

For some, interrogating the argument is uncomfortable. Critique is taken as personal criticism, more likely so by the champion of a project. In fact, if well handled, the converse is true. Critique not only strengthens the argument, it attracts greater involvement. The more individuals have dug deep, the greater the likelihood of commitment from the board, especially when the going gets tough.

"Cutting off discussion; exhibiting impatience with questioning. They are the worst behaviours from a chairman," says Michael Chaney.

It is as disconcerting for a board to deduce that the CEO does not have the full backing of his or her team, as it is for the management to witness the chairman browbeating board members to a pre-agreed position. At some point in the future the project is likely to come under pressure. Confidence that the board will continue to provide support is undermined. A half hearted, "yes, I support it" is more damaging than "rethink this proposal."

Positioning the argument

How boards work in practice varies. But an evidence-based proposition with argument is a primary requirement of decision making. Additionally, any major project needs championing. Being the champion is a passionate affair. (Think back to our earlier discussion about the importance of passion. The boardroom, for all the reverence and mahogany, is a passionate place.) Strong bonding with the initiative and the people involved, is natural. Hidden beneath a clearly thought through argument are powerful emotions. Scrutinizing any case requires attention to logic but also to relationships so that the coherent logic underlying the argument prevails without undermining the passion for success.

In verbalizing the argument, the manner of conversation needs consideration. Is it dialogue or debate? A great deal depends on the depth of understanding desired by the parties involved. The psychological contract with each other has to be appreciated as, so often, that determines the quality of outcome of the debate process.

David Clarke describes the interrogation of a strategic proposal submission to the board of Macquarie Bank. The discussion was penetrating and challenging.

We heard the case. The board members asked me, 'Are you happy with this?' – to which I said, 'Happy for you to see it and the CEO knows that.' We questioned and concluded that it was pretty good but the argument needed tightening. So back it went – when can you have it ready? Next meeting? OK, we look forward to that.

The argument underlying the proposal was thoroughly examined. The case was improved through revision, which, in turn, strengthened commitment to action. "The management team agreed that they benefited from the revision. Board and management are strengthened and are absolutely clear about that," notes Clarke. "We all gained. The analysis was so penetrating, all identified with the outcome. All are committed to the plan of action."

Managing expectations

One of the most important aspects of the chairman's role is to set the context for board discussion. How an argument is introduced and the signals from the chairman can make a huge difference. In particular, the chairman can either defuse a highly charged atmosphere – or light the fuse. Key to this is the understanding that the chairman has with the CEO.

"The chief executive should feel free to contact the chairman anytime, any hour, day or night," says Pat Molloy. Michael Chaney observes: "Having a good relationship with the CEO is very important. I think chemistry is all about that."

As we have emphasized throughout, a positive relationship between chairman and CEO is crucial. Words such as openness, trust, and respect are used to describe a productive and fruitful relationship. Yet these words are *dyadic*, capturing the intimacy of the relationship between the two people. What about the quality of relationships at meetings, where comment and countercomment are the reality within a setting of a group?

Terms such as robustness and resilience are more appropriate. The relationship between the chairman and CEO is no love in. "I try to make it clear to management how they should present their case, what they should expect from the board and what is the benefit of the board. Clear and transparent – no surprises – people know how to use each other and gain benefit from each other," says Vadim Makhov.

Vadim Makhov refers to the positioning of expectations. Quality of evidence, structure of argument, and attention to detail are essential ingredients to gaining approval of the case put to the board. There is a final consideration and that is the positioning of expectations. How should the case be viewed? Surfacing with a positive view from the board members in order to achieve desired outcomes requires the chairman to mold the thinking of both management and the board. This requires a personal and sensitive touch.

There are no universals in this. As we have seen, particular trends concerning board orientation prevail. More common in the United States and United Kingdom is for the board to vet the strategy and vision presented by the CEO and the management. For reasons more due to the unique geography of Australia, the board more proactively determines strategy and vision. Equally, for reasons of history and positioning in the economic life cycle, the family shareholding structure of Turkey places the chairman in a pivotal position driving strategy and vision.

Each board determines its own purpose. As Lord Sandy Bruce Lockhart emphasizes, contrary to UK custom, the vision may well be driven by the chairman. The distinguishing factor is strength of personality; who overrides who?

The danger of such idiosyncrasy is that it can lead to unwelcome tension. Role delineation determines that it is the chairman who positions the nature of the contribution of the board. To not make that clear undermines management and their positioning of proposals for board consideration. The chairman sets the scene outlining how the board is to work but also how it is to listen. Providing background and setting expectations toward a proposal enables the board to appreciate reasoning. Why are we discussing this proposal in the first case? Not only are the reasons for the proposal made clear but so too are the assumptions underlying the design of the case.

George Bell, former KPMG partner, invited to chair Anglia Farmers UK, the merger of two farming cooperatives, prepared his board through exposure to the strategic and operational thinking of the management.

> I was very concerned that the board should know something, at least of what was going on in the business, rather than just swanning in from outside for monthly board meetings. Historically, they would have had the accountant come in and tell them how they were doing. Thus, the chap who looked after fertiliser would come in and talk about the fertiliser market and the girl who looked after chemicals would come in and do the same thing.

"This is completely pointless," commented George Bell.

> management simply tell the board what they want them to hear. I expect directors, working in teams of two, to understand the key areas of the business well enough to brief the board on their area. This can be challenging, particularly because some of the directors hadn't quite learnt the fact that they are not there to manage the business, they are there to provide direction.

Through clarifying for the board the thinking and assumptions made by management, emphasizes the challenges management face. The board is now 'realistic' in its deliberation.

The chairman's guidance of the challenges facing management assists the board to realistically assess the merits of the case put before them. Setting stretching expectations and targets is motivational. Requiring impossible hurdles to be met deteriorates the performance of management. Of course, what is stretching for one is viewed as impossible by the other, often for no other reason than who does the determining. However, it is up to the chairman and the board to distinguish when stretching become damaging. Without providing a contextual overview of what management continuously face, board members refer to another reality, another board, another management, another organization, in effect, a reality of somewhere else.

"Different boards are effective in different ways," concludes Rosalind Gilmore. She is unquestionably right and making use of that versatility requires being grounded in the challenges of the organization on whose board the directors sit. The worst notion to hold is of a success somewhere else, which makes success over here impossible to achieve.

As the chairman positions the board to be receptive to the argument from management, he or she also briefs management concerning board expectation and mind-set.

An overview of the thinking of the board is a good place to start.

- What issues capture the board's attention?
- Does the board hold concerns over the organization and its management and, if so, what are these?
- Is the board ready to listen to the case at hand?

Appropriately positioning the case requires guidance on how to present the proposition to the board. In so doing, the chairman should specify his or her position – support of the case or that the case is now worthy of the board's scrutiny. Alternatively, one should go back and rework the presentation. The chairman's interrogation of the briefing to be given to the board assists management to appreciate the board's level of receptivity.

Discussing the issues

Positioning the argument, positioning the board, and positioning the management draw out open and robust dialogue. A clear brief precedes a conclusive outcome. All involved have been prepared. Politics is minimized.

Rosalind Gilmore provides a characteristically pithy summary: "continuity, coherence and competence." These three "c's" specify the capabilities required of management in positioning their case to the board.

The first "c" is "continuity" keep the board updated and in touch. Says Rosalind Gilmore, "Management need to understand that you have not been living in their minds and pockets for the last six weeks. They actually have to keep you in touch." But, how do management keep the board in touch? "Locate the key issues when you turn up. The pre-reading needs to support that." From the start, one should clearly focus the board's attention on what management consider being the prime issues for consideration.

The second "c" – "coherence" – refers to shared understanding. Rosalind Gilmore explains: "I don't mean everybody agrees. But I do mean that they understand each other and understand what each other is saying. I think first and foremost, it is down to the chairman to help us to get to know each other."

Rosalind Gilmore refers to uninhibited conversation and teamwork. The theme of working together is taken further by David Pumphrey, partner of Heidrick and Struggles in Australia. He champions the level and quality of teamwork on Australian boards. "It's in the culture. It's part of the psyche," he says. For David Pumphrey, teamwork is a key distinguishing characteristic of high-performing boards as long as the focus is on the coherence of the argument and not on behavioral niceties.

The third "c" is "competence." The chairman's briefing of management to take account of the board's response to the proposals put before them involves outlining the competences of each board member. "Competence does mean that everybody brings something to the table and that taken cumulatively is something substantial," says Rosalind Gilmore.

Dialogue or debate?

In our study, so many chairmen, CEOs, and other board members used the term *debate* to describe the intensity of the conversation. A minority offered an alternative view.

"You should understand people. You make sure that all basic opinions are taken into account. Everyone around the table learns. Through real sharing of opinion, people better understand and communicate well," Vadim Makhov told us.

This alternative view is captured in the term *dialogue*. Vadim Makhov makes reference to dialogue, not debate. While the terms dialogue and debate are used interchangeably, in fact the difference between them is considerable.

Dialogue goes back to ancient Greece, Socrates in particular. Socrates, philosopher, orator, teacher, and one of the most formidable intellectuals of his day, wrote nothing. Plato wrote Socrates. What we have is Socrates, second hand. Through Plato, Socratic philosophy has influenced generations, particularly in forms of oratory.[4] Socrates championed dialogue, not debate, for the purposes of achieving diligent inquiry. Socrates' unique contribution to the art of rhetoric is about reasoning; the construction of an argument and refutation of argument being a collaborative rather than an adversarial experience. In Socratic dialogue, no one wins, but all are engaged. The search is for the very best argument. Very best is determined according to circumstance and context.

What is the best supportive case? What are the very best of objections? As Vadim Makhov emphasizes, learning has to totally encompass the individual and the group, the essence of Socratic philosophy.

The term dialogue comes from two Greek roots, *dia* meaning flowing through and *logo* meaning the clarifying of assumptions and mental modes, in keeping with today's commonly made interpretation of *logos* being the word, the word of God, or the ultimate statement. Through dialogue, the champion of an initiative encourages uninhibited examination, requesting that colleagues adopt counterpositions in order to explore what part of the argument put forward could survive. "Look at the world from the other point of view; see if it makes sense!" they challenge. During dialogue, all discussants act as champions of 360° interrogation in order to have the confidence in the components of the argument that survive discourse. No one loses; everyone wins. The emphasis is on ceaseless conversation, which can involve negotiation, compromise, mutual exploration, and inquiry, with the cycle repeating itself many times over.

Sounds simple enough, but not according to Socrates. For Socrates, dialogue is a state of mind not a mode of conversation. Such a state of mind is not easily realized. More common is debate, a particularly English innovation captured in the very structure of the House of Commons, the lower chamber of the United Kingdom's Houses of Parliament. Debate denotes beating down, breaking the argument of the other side. Debate requires taking sides and confrontation. The side that wins, wins the argument. Winning and not necessarily emerging with the best case, distinguishes debate from dialogue. Winning can be based on strength of argument. Winning can also be entirely dependent on undermining the case of the other side, worst still, discrediting the other side, rather than paying attention to improving one's own case. Debate could also mean bullying. The loudest voice wins irrespective of the prevailing logic.

In the boardroom, understanding the difference between debate and dialogue is vital, if the arguments put forward are to be truly interrogated, understood, and acted on.

Drawing out value from the board necessitates consideration of the value to gain from each board member. If nothing else, consideration of each board member is an evident display of respect for the board.

Now, argument and counterargument are exposed. The best in Socratic dialogue is visibly experienced. Apart from greater efficiency of decision making, the learning that ensues is immeasurable. The alternative is defense and attack with the accompanying danger that the loudest voice wins.

Reworking the argument

"It is perfectly proper to ask management to rework the case if it falls short of our analysis," says Ishak Alaton. "If the proposition does not survive board deliberation, send it back" is the view put forward by David Clarke of Macquarie Bank.

There is no shame in reworking the case. Indeed, it is often necessary. Ultimately all benefit. But, our research shows that many share this view but few practice it. The majority admit to caution in presenting a case to the board that may not survive their scrutiny. If the case is poor, then caution to proceed is understandable. If the relationships between the chairman and CEO, between board members, and/or between the board and management are dysfunctional it is understandable that caution arises. On the management side, all too often propositions never reach the board for fear of rejection, not because the case is weak but because the board is not ready. It is the chairman's responsibility to improve the workings of the board. Anomalies on the board dull management's enthusiasm and proactivity.

David Pumphrey's assertion that teamwork on boards is healthy holds weight. A smart working board, drawing together their skills of interrogation, requesting that management reconsider their proposition, is not a sign of failure. It is a clear indication of a healthy and vibrant board. However, blatantly sending a case back to management to rethink is unhelpful. Effectively reworking the argument requires guidance, involvement, and support from the chairman and the board. Observation of high performing boards draws attention to four parameters for reworking the argument:

No shame culture

Loss of face, loss of credibility, even shame; these are the experiences described by both management and board directors when proposals are rejected or returned requiring further deliberation. The two who most feel sensitive are the chairman and CEO. But why? Assuming that open and transparent deliberation brings to the surface valuable suggestions for improvement to the original proposal, why then should there be negative emotions?

Dialogue requires examination of the case from all angles. Identifying improvements contributes greatly to the longer-term sustainability of the proposal. There is no shame in being asked to improve an already well thought through case. Einstein, one of the outstanding minds of the twentieth century, did not publish much, but what he did publish was in academic journals, which required what is called *blind peer review*. Unknown fellow

academics confidentially critiqued his papers. The response to
Einstein was, revise and resubmit – your work is great but there
is room for improvement. Imagine the twentieth century if
Einstein had sulked and said, "no, to hell with you, accept what
I have submitted or nothing at all!" Perfecting the proposal goes
hand in hand with a robustness and personal resilience to challenge, listen, and counterchallenge. Pushing for open and in-
depth conversation leads to a no shame culture. David Clarke
suggests that through having the right culture on the board, all
learn, all benefit. He also acknowledges that such a board is
not for the faint hearted.

No pet themes

Nurturing a no blame culture demands objectivity and impartiality from board members. What undermines a positive and
progressive approach to conversation is the pursuit of pet
themes.

Helen Nellis, former chairman of the United Kingdom's
Bedfordshire Health Authority says:

> There was a tendency to look at things from individual exper-
> iences, you know my granny had a bad experience with her
> hip, or something and we were asked to extrapolate from
> that, that all grannies have bad experiences with their hips.
> We've really got to fight against this approach and create
> strategy on analysis of good information.

Taking into account the contextual pressures management faces
aids scrutiny of the proposal. Board members who have had
other contextual experiences, unless directly relevant, should be
omitted from the conversation. There is a natural tendency to
refer to powerful, personal experiences as the benchmark for
determining the merits of a case. The solution? Helen Nellis suggests: "It's about understanding the role. They [board members]
are there to bring diverse perspectives and it's about feeding
those into the bigger picture and not simply relying on an individual's interpretation of single events."

A prime requirement of the chairman is to ensure the board draws on relevant, timely, and rationally considered evidence.

Criteria for reworking

"We identify those areas that need reworking. We especially give attention to the criteria for re-submission. Our job is to support and provide for the best possible solution," says Macquarie's David Clarke.

David Clark goes on to clarify the reasons for sending back proposals. These are as follows:

- to tighten the argument;
- to amend the actual deal – price, conditions, safeguards, and so on;
- for more data on areas where the proposal is, perhaps, silent;
- for better justification of important assertions.

He goes on to say, "they then come back in amended form, and are then usually approved, but sometimes they don't, especially if management doesn't think that it can satisfy the board's reservations."

What needs improving? Only those specific areas that require attention. Clarifying what further work needs reconsideration goes hand in hand with identifying the criteria for determining the quality of the resubmission. Clarity of project submission and resubmission has paid dividends for Macquarie Bank. It has been transformed from the Australian branch of London's Hill Samuel, to become a global player with a portfolio of A$89 billion and 7000 people in 23 countries.[5]

The original leadership team of Alan Moss as CEO and David Clarke as chairman are still in post.[6] Their leadership, focus, and stringency have produced a remarkably long lasting partnership. In Australia, the average period of tenure for a CEO is reported as four years. On this basis, Alan Moss considers himself as approaching "250 years old."

Realistic time frames

By when should the proposal be resubmitted? Setting an achievable time frame for resubmission requires appreciation of the depth of work needed. That clarity should be reached between chairman and CEO and then agreed by the board. In the rare circumstances of further time being required, tracking progress is down to the chairman's follow through with the CEO.

Key points

- Constructively interrogating the argument ensures successful adoption of the proposal, reduces risk, and safeguards the reputation of the organization.
- Constructive argument interrogation increases the commitment of board and management to the project.
- The chairman together with management should break down the argument into its constituent parts so as to gain the full attention of the board.
- In breaking down the argument, the chairman coaches management to emphasize the relevance, alignment, quality of supporting evidence, and logical sequencing of the argument.
- The chairman determines the quality of discussion in verbalizing the argument. The consideration is one of dialogue or debate. Dialogue encourages in-depth, uninhibited exploration, whereas debate induces win or lose and the taking of sides for and against, so that the most powerful presence in the room carries the case, irrespective of whether that is the best argument.
- The psychological contract between chairman and CEO, chairman and board, and board and management clarifies the parameters for challenge to the proposition before the board.
- The chairman prepares the board to appreciate the intricacies and details of the proposition by informing the

→

board of relevant strategic and operational developments and also of the challenges facing management.

- The chairman briefs management to appropriately position their argument through emphasizing the issues dominating the board's attention and of their level of preparedness to listen.
- Adopting the 3 c's framework of continuity, coherence, and competence guides management to position their case so as to draw the best out of the board.
- Reworking the proposition should be viewed as a gain, not damage or failure.
- Reworking the argument for the purposes of an improved outcome requires the chairman to establish a no shame culture at board and senior management levels, emphasizing objectivity, impartiality, clear criteria for reworking the case, and realistic time frames for resubmission. Promoting a pet theme by one or more board member(s) undermines the no shame culture.

Influencing outcomes

> If you listen carefully and you've got a finger on the pulse of the board, you can influence actions and thoughts. Plan a little ahead and talk about this. Clever, thoughtful people expect direction as long as concerns are addressed.
>
> Viscount Etienne Davignon,
> vice chairman of Suez-Tractebel,
> chairman CMB

When we interviewed him, Viscount Davignon referred frequently to the different perspectives offered by his colleagues on the board. He was aware of and had respect for their views. Views require airing. The wisdom and experience of each board member needs capturing. Showing respect for each director's independence while at the same time harnessing the range of opinions expressed into a cohesive contribution requires personal sensitivity. It also requires the clarity of mind to work towards desired outcomes. The fourth discipline of the effective chairman is the skill of influencing in order to realize particular goals. That is the focus of this chapter.

There is an important distinction to be drawn here between influencing outcomes, which is what we are concerned with, and driving through outcomes, which is an altogether more aggressive approach liable to create ill feeling and discontent.

Influencing outcomes is a subtle art. An independent director of a US company (who preferred to remain anonymous) expressed admiration for one chairman who knowingly influenced his colleagues to satisfy his predetermined ends. The same director also expressed his distaste for being pushed into supporting a particular decision, while having been a member of another board. The more blatant pushing induced confrontation between the board and the chairman. In both circumstances, the intentions of the chairman were clear. The difference was the manner in which those intentions were achieved.

"He knows what he wants and he just tries to bully it through," said the director. "This is going to lead to a bust up. Not like another board on which I sit where we all know what the chairman wants, but he achieves it with style. It's a pleasure to be guided to where the chairman wanted us in the first place."

Skillful influencing requires *appropriateness* of style. Consideration of the unique nature of each circumstance and adjustment to the individuals on the board, taking into account the perspective of each member, allows for a focusing of energy toward a particular outcome. In fact, influencing to achieve particular objectives requires as much logical analysis as it does swaying people's views one way or another.

Our research identified five steps toward effective influencing:

1. **The surfacing of sentiments.** The chairman has to draw to the surface what board members really feel about the board, the management, and the organization, the way issues are being dealt with, and about each other as colleagues. Such admissions are inevitably accompanied by tense sentiments. Why such a volatile cocktail bubbles under the boardroom surface is discussed. Having drawn to the surface those powerful but hidden emotions that can undermine decisions reached, the next step involves the strength to work through sentiments.

2. **The strength to work through divisive emotions.** In fact, personal resilience acts as the platform for the next step.

3. **Oratory skill.** Oratory skill without strength of character is viewed as sophistry. But when force of conviction and persuasive speech are brought together, the message becomes potent. Language and tone of voice cleverly handled allow the most sensitive of conversations to take place.

4. **Focusing on the salient points in the debate.** Powerful individuals enmeshed in demanding discussion can unwittingly divert the conversation down a number of unproductive avenues. One of the skills of chairmanship is to draw the group back to the key point of discussion.

5. **Thinking several meetings ahead.** Like an accomplished chess player, the effective chairman thinks several moves ahead. The world-class chairman is akin to the Grand Master. He knows all the gambits and has played out the boardroom strategies many times. This involves the positioning of deliberating meetings ahead of time to mold expectations of the considerations under scrutiny. In effect, it is a way of ensuring that the chairman carries the board with him.

Surfacing sentiments

The board needs to fully engage. The issue under debate is contentious. The discussion is likely to be uncomfortable. Yet, in order to move forward, a shared view has to be achieved. The chairman, through his or her skills of personal influence, guides the discussion to a point where a unanimous decision is reached. Despite expressed commitment to the decision, the chairman and possibly other directors have the feeling that not all are as committed as they publicly state.

Is this situation unusual? No, far from it: our international research spanning many thousands of organizations indicates that these sorts of difficult and sensitive discussion are a regular although unwelcome experience for most executives, even the more seasoned ones (Table 4.1).

The level of inhibition at senior management levels is high. Thirty-six percent of top French managers to 80 percent of top Chinese managers and officials of private sector and state

Table 4.1 Feeling inhibited[a]

	Japan	United Kingdom	France	Ireland	Germany	Sweden	Spain
%	77	47	36	68	61	50	63

	Austria	Finland	United States	China	Hong Kong	NHS	Australia
%	67	49	62	80	58	66	66

Note: NHS: National Health Service.

[a] Further information on sensitivity of dialogue is found in A. Kakabadse and N. Kakabadse (1999), *Essence of Leadership*, London. International Thomson Business Press, p. 324.

organizations admit to backing down from airing uncomfortable but pertinent issues. We have seen that one-third of the world's
organizations have senior managers who hold undeclared, but
nevertheless, deeply held differences of view concerning the
vision, mission, and future of the organization (see Table 2.1). In
addition, approximately two-thirds of the world's top executives
find it difficult to address relevant but sensitive issues.

Such was the case with a European pharmaceutical company.
The newly appointed CEO concluded that the company's structure and product and services portfolio required redesign.
Divestment of certain product families and less profitable subsidiaries and divisions was agreed first with the management
team and then with the board. At board discussions the management presented a united front. However, a minority of board
members felt that not only was the strategy of repositioning the
firm suspect but also that members of the management team
were not wholly convinced of their argument. Certain board
members held private discussions with the chairman, but that
led nowhere. One of the American directors, at a subsequent
board meeting, raised the question of rethinking the restructuring of the group, but to no avail. The chairman dampened the
discussion.

Over the next few months, it became slowly evident that deep
disaffection existed at senior management levels. Key business
heads and support function directors were challenging the CEO
at executive committee meetings. Further, two high profile res-
ignations led to further speculation of a divided and troubled
top management. Matters came to a head when the relatively
newly appointed group marketing director labeled the group's
branding and pricing strategy as unrealistic. These disagree-
ments came to the attention of board members, who, themselves,
were well tuned into the organization. At the next board meeting they expressed their concerns about the leadership capacity
of the CEO and also about the damage to the reputation of the
organization as stories of managerial strife began to float to
influential journalists. Still the chairman supported the CEO.

The underlying tensions at board level came to the surface at a
dinner the evening prior to a board meeting. The most senior of

the independent directors raised the issue of damaging tensions and poor leadership. Why, the director asked, was the board not discussing reputational risk and managerial incompetence? The level of unease among the board members was evident. The chairman agreed that the senior colleague who raised the concern should canvass the opinions of the other board members. The chairman learnt that not only was the leadership of the organization a concern but so was the chairman's tendency to suppress bad news. Greater involvement from the board is required – was the clear message. The chairman declared surprise. The lack of trust in the CEO was nothing new; the concern about the chairman's style was.

To the chairman's credit, he did listen. To the surprise of board members, he made stringent efforts to adapt his style of running the board. The chairman's change of style was met with admiration and positive comment. The lapses into sullen silence that had dogged previous board meetings quickly evaporated. Concerns over strategy and what was generally happening in the organization were given a full airing. More open discussion not only led to more fruitful discourse but genuine support for the chairman. It was agreed that the chair should explore with the CEO the strategic direction being pursued as well as the CEO's style of management. The chairman reported to the board that the CEO remained convinced that he was on the right track and had argued his case strongly. The chairman reiterated the CEO's strategy to the board which, within the new culture of more in-depth discussion, they more readily accepted. However, concern remained over the CEO's style. Unwilling to change, the CEO left amicably to be replaced by an individual whose demeanor was favorably received by both board and management. Ironically, the same strategy is currently being pursued but with a different CEO who displays a more welcoming approach.

Is this an unusual story? Not really. In molding the future for the organization, leaders display not only their rational, analytical side but also their philosophy and style. When concerns about strategy reach board level, suppression of either simply stores up problems for the future. Inadequate examination of either leaves the organization vulnerable. A poorly functioning board monitors badly. Further, commitment to and ownership of any decision reached is also low. What makes things worse is that board directors and top management know what is wrong and what is needed to put things right.

Through surfacing underlying sentiments, all the insights ever needed to address the concerns and challenges facing the organization are present and available. There are no secrets at the levels of board and top management. One distinguished US director, sitting on the board of a major UK organization, explained why the high profile collapse of his company occurred:

> It was basically the weakness of the chairman. He should have got hold of those two warring directors and said, enough – work together or one or both go. But he did not. What is worse is he manipulated us, the board. Whenever we raised the issue of tension between these two top managers, he took each one of us, separately, to dinner and persuaded us that this [the tension between the two top managers] was nothing. As a person, the chairman was charming. Over dinner we felt better. But not the next day. And so it went on until – well the rest of the story you know.

Why do deeply held tensions arise? From our research, we identified five sources of boardroom tension:

1. **Level of director involvement.** "I cannot tell you how important it is to let the independent directors have their say," says James Parkel. "To resist that is like inviting cancerous tissue to spread."

"I go round the board table and I ensure that everyone debates an issue," says Don Argus, chairman of BHP Billiton. "I get their views on the issue. Everyone will debate from their position of strength and from their skill strength. Now that we have everyone's position, we need to debate an outcome and give management the lead as to whether the board supports the issue or not."

Don Argus is clear. Boards are elected by the shareholders to represent their interests. It is from this perspective that openness and depth of debate is necessary.

"The skill is reaching that desired level of commitment," adds Kelly O'Dea, chairman of AllianceHPL. As O'Dea outlines, the purpose of full and frank discourse is depth of scrutiny and commitment to the decision reached.

The message is crystal clear: involve the board. But many chairmen fail to achieve this.

2. **Quality of director contribution.** Why is each of the board directors at the table? At the time of appointment, what was the intended role and contribution of each? Has each contributed as expected? These are common place questions that naturally induce a different response for each board director on each board.

The greatest contrast of response is witnessed on US boards (Table 4.2). Overall, US chairmen, more than those from other countries, paint a favorable picture of life on their board. In public, a similar positive picture is portrayed by independent directors. Yet, in private, independent directors offer the greatest contrast of views concerning the reality of life on the board. Few deny that inhibition influences thinking and behavior on the board and on the management team. The key difference with all others is the quality of contribution. Of American independent directors who consider their board as an average performer more report that they are considerably underutilized. Whatever the original reason for being offered a position on the board, they describe their level of influence as "limited."

In many cases, the story is of a board and organization driven by an imperial chairman/CEO. Those board directors that hold

Table 4.2   US boards: contract of contributors

Average board	Best-led board
• Inhibition	• Reduced inhibition
• Defensiveness	• Speak more openly
• Limited influence (unless celebrity)	• Influential
• Limited use of strengths	• Link skills of director to strategy
• Discouraged from talking to staff/ management	• Robust dialogue
• Imperial chairman/CEO	• Chair/CEO actively invites comment
• Few good candidates	• Deluge of candidates

celebrity status are viewed as favorites of the chairman/CEO. They are invited to comment more frequently and their views are listened to and acknowledged. None of this is a secret, as poor performing boards are well known in the sector and in the networks. The number of candidates expressing interest in vacant board positions is minimal.

Comments one American independent director: "Not being used well affects all aspects of the board. People do not contribute. Tensions arise. Out of duty, I turn up to meetings. I know the chairman thinks I do not contribute but when I do nothing happens. I blame him. He blames me. The board goes nowhere."

Drawing out the best from the board is the responsibility of the chairman. One poor performing board member may be the result of a wrong appointment. Continual unsatisfactory performance and contribution is down to the chairman.

"Do you know for how long being a poor board and not fully taking part can go on for – well – years. Or at least, that is what is happening on our board," confides one independent director on an American board.

Poor contribution can become a habit. A chairman who is poor at drawing out the best from board colleagues becomes accustomed to not being challenged. Chairman and board members form a dysfunctionally comfortable relationship. The board racks up costs but offers little value. Worse still, vulnerabilities creep in, undermining the organization.

In sharp contrast, American boards that are considered to be well led are described as an integral part of a successful organization. Inevitably, tensions exist but speaking openly and visibly contributing are integral to the culture of the board. The majority of independent directors consider themselves as making a positive contribution. The link between each director's skills and experience and the role they are asked to play on the board is evident. Strong interest is expressed from capable and experienced directors for vacant positions on well-led boards.

A universal truth is that the explicit purpose of boards is to monitor, to audit but also support management. From there on, the quality of director contributions is partly determined by each individual director, partly by the skills and style of the chairman and partly by the implicit purpose of the board. Not surprising therefore, our research identifies differences of practice. As we have seen, Australian boards have slightly different dynamics – thanks to geographic isolation, the increasing habit of hiring top managers from abroad, and the greater dominance of the Australian chairman. Australian boards monitor, audit, and support as others but also more determine the vision of the organization and take a commanding role in driving the strategy. For reasons of family shareholding structures, Turkish chairmen, often the majority shareholder, drive strategy and determines the vision, similar to the Australian firm. In contrast, British boards and chairmen emerge as more passive.

But these are overall trends. The two critical units are the board and the chairman. Each is unique and it is the strength of personality of the chairman that shapes board purpose and functionality. Hence, an additional reason for dysfunctional board dynamics and less than satisfactory contribution is low shared understanding of the purpose of the board. A CEO dominated by a powerful chairman is unlikely to fully contribute, being reduced to playing out the role of COO. Unable to redress what should be the purpose of the board, the more capable directors resign.

Resigning is not undertaken lightly as, through so doing, the ills of the company are brought to public view. Resigning can tarnish the image of the person within the network. Affiliations are damaged and, even today, affiliation emerges as the prime reason for board appointments despite governance codes and the increased professionalism of headhunters. A considerable number of directors admitted that the greatest challenge they faced was resigning from one or other board.

Worse than resignation is to have those less capable remain on the board. The resignation of the more able, levers the way for an over dominant chairman (or CEO) to bully the board into accepting candidates who are unlikely to challenge the status quo.

3. **Boundary delineation.** As we have seen, another area of poor role boundary determination is that of the senior independent director (SID). Contrived as the last port of call for disgruntled shareholders, numerous SIDs have professed to not knowing what they should be doing on the board that is any different to what they did prior to being endowed with senior status. Publicly, no such concerns are expressed. Privately and to varying degrees, confusion and distress are reported.

"I am doing what the rest of us as a board should be doing" commented one SID. He continued, "I am really policing the chairman, who is policing the CEO, who is being scrutinized by the shareholders, who turn to me if they cannot get anywhere. By which time, it is too late!"

Despite frustration, few SIDs have resigned. Privately, some admit that they would damage their personal reputation should they do so.

4. **Differences of view.** Differences of view between directors, especially when reported in the business media, raise tensions that can undermine the board. However, our research highlights that differences of view are not the main concern for the board and the chairman. At least, directors are talking about the key challenges facing the board. Challenge, even confrontation can be uncomfortable but tension, of itself, is no bad thing. Directors resigning because of transparent differences of view do not bankrupt the organization and rarely damage the board. The language used may be colorful and dramatic but life goes on. One director leaving because of genuine differences of view more often than not leads to opportunities: the opportunity to rethink and the opportunity to find a replacement and strengthen the board. Suppressed tension is the concern. Problems that should be addressed continuing and remaining unchallenged can cause irreparable harm.

5. **The chemistry factor.** More potent than differences of view is the chemistry factor. As we have seen, chemistry is elusive but deeply important. One should ask the following questions:

- Can we relate?
- Can we work together?

- Do we share the same interests?
- Are we of a like mind?

Whether chemistry refers to a sharing of interests, background, experience of values or personality, the bonding of chemistry is tested by the capacity between the parties to interpret information and events in a similar manner. Not interpreting the world in a comparable manner can be partly compensated for by friendship or what the ancient Greeks termed as *philos*, namely friend. Lacking the philos dimension as well as the sharing of thinking and interpretation, leads to despising and disrespect – the board director's nightmare.

Unwilling to be identified, one independent director described the almost unworkable strains on her board:

> I think the chief executive is great – so, too, is the chairman. But there is contempt between them. The chairman gets stuck into the CEO. The chairman is not liked by the other board members but at least they respect his abilities. No such respect is evident from the CEO. On balance the relationship is just about workable because the chief exec tries really hard and just ignores the crap. How long this can continue, well that is another matter!

In fact, the tension continued for another 20 months. In the intervening period, rumors of rifts on the board were denied. The reputation of the board and the organization was slowly tarnished. The share price dropped but not dramatically. No acquisitions were pursued. To the press, media, and shareholders, the overall impression was of an organization in stagnation.

Strangely, bad chemistry sometimes evokes greater professionalism. "The chairman and I are polite to each other. We have little more and even that is hard work," explains the CEO of one European company.

> One day, I was tired, irritable, stretched in too many directions and I nearly lost my cool. I managed to keep myself restrained. Had I not that would have caused a complete breakdown in our relationship. The result would have been a

catastrophe. It is just what the press ad media would have
wanted. The relationship cannot get better no matter how
hard we both try. We are both professional. The question is:
who will go first?

The effort required to maintain a publicly respectful relationship in the full knowledge that little value is being created is
considerable. The important point is that the organization
should function; the board should do its job, and the management should get on with running the business.

What is surprising is for how long incompatible relationships
continue. Some justify continuing with an apparently unworkable relationship on the board as needing to find the right time
to depart. Others find the challenge of facing up to personal
confrontation too daunting. Despite the recognition that one of
the erring parties should depart, it is, for many, emotionally
easier to continue. Facing an emotionally damaging relationship is deeply discomforting, particularly when the likely
response from the other party is denial.

"I have known many chairmen, CEOs and board members try
and find, or create, the right time to talk things through in a
professional and calm manner," says Tom Sawyer.

> It rarely works. What you end up doing is using your skills
> and experience to keep something going that should have
> died ages ago. The best thing to do is make up your mind,
> you are going to face the situation. It's messy and uncom-
> fortable but go through it. The relief afterwards is great.

Working through divisive emotions

Drawing to the surface what is bubbling under the surface is the
first step to influencing outcomes on the board. Harnessing
powerful sentiments can have an astoundingly positive effect.
Deny the presence of powerful emotions and the outcome is a
continued slow deterioration of board and organizational performance. But once the first step has been accomplished then

the skilled chairman moves onto the second step: using his or her personal strength to work through these sentiments.

Working through sentiments is no easy matter. Considerable resilience and discipline is needed to proceed with what is an emotionally draining experience.

We return to Tom Sawyer's uncomfortable experience with one of his former CEOs.

> Well, I suppose this is a human failing but I actually liked the bloke. ... I got him a mentor. I sent him off to business school. I did everything that I could to have faith in him because I thought he was a worthy man. I believed he needed every opportunity to prove himself and in the end he did not.

Facing up to the problem, Tom Sawyer sat down with his CEO to confront the issue of performance. "I told him, he had to go. There was no backing out. One, he could resign. Two, he could be sacked. Sensibly, he resigned and got out with some dignity."

Reflecting on his experience, Tom Sawyer comments: "I spent too much time trying to make it work. I learnt from that not to get too close. I won't make that mistake again."

Needing to influence outcomes as a result of leading through change or pressing for performance improvement requires a robustness to work through tense emotions. There are no guarantees. Despite personal qualities, the individual could lose out and be forced to leave. However, not to draw out the deeply held sentiments on the board or in the management team guarantees that nothing will change.

This brings us to step 3, the personal skills of influencing.

Oratory skills

"It's all about listening and then knowing how to address each issue bearing in mind the personalities on the board," says a US CEO/president referring to the ability to judge the level of receptivity of each of the board members. It is a skill born of listening, flexibility of style, and sensitivity.

"Yes you have to listen and yes you have to be sensitive to your colleagues," says Bernard Rethore. "But then you need a repertoire of styles, sometimes direct opposites to each other. You need to encourage discussion and then other times cut through. You need to be warm and yet tough. So much depends on timing and knowing your colleagues." A contrast of styles needs to be drawn on. Knowing what to use with whom and when is vital.

What you say and how you say it are fundamental. The capability to span speech forms is a phenomenon that has been deeply scrutinized and admired by philosophers.

Socrates proposed dialogue as the speech form for sustained democratic discourse (see Discipline 3, Dialogue or Debate). Agile in question and answer, the Socratic mode of conversation was perfected by Aristotle. The Aristotelian version of dialogue passed to Persia, Africa, Spain, France, and then to England. The English champion of dialogue was Francis Bacon, philosopher and scientist and one of the first empiricists. Bacon molded the chaotic nature of dialogue into rational, systematic argument, drawing on data. Through Bacon, observation, induction, and deduction have become the principles of research for the last few hundred years.

English rationalism draws from one side of Socrates. There was another, a slightly different branch of getting at the truth, that of dialectics (*dialegos* in ancient Greek means discourse).[1] It was the German philosophers, Kant, Hegel, and later Karl Marx who incorporated dialectics into their thinking. Dialectics requires reaching in-depth understanding through taking, for a while, the opposite view during conversation. In this way, the merits of each case become crystal clear. Each individual not only champions their view but also immerses themselves in the opposite camp in order to appreciate their position. In effect, dialectics is a more intensive and scrutinising form of dialogue.

In the 1970s, the scientific discipline of Francis Bacon and the dialectical sophistication of Marx were combined by one of the great scholars to come out of the Frankfurt school of philosophy,

Habermas. Habermas recognized that a scientific rational approach to conversation is fine, but how to use it? How does one pursue dialogue and dialectics? Habermas examined the relationship between speech and reflection. He concluded that all too often, people intend to adopt dialogue but end up debating. They offer – in fact, push – their view. Habermas warned not to confuse displays of enthusiasm with commitment. On the day and at the meeting, it is all too easy to misinterpret boisterous rapture for long-term dedication and staying power.

To redress the disadvantages of one way conversation, no matter how nicely phrased, Habermas offers a common set of speech guidelines: listen; speak without judgment; acknowledge the other speaker; respect difference; suspend using role and status to influence; avoid cross talking; and focus on learning.

Habermas took these guidelines and evolved four speech forms, framing/re-framing, advocating, illustrating, and inquiry (Table 4.3).

Table 4.3 Habermas's speech forms

Speech forms	Involves	Why use	Example
Framing/reframing	Not assuming that others hold similar focus of reference	Appreciate better others awareness, mind-set, vision, questions, anxiety	"What does leadership mean for you?"
Advocating	Rationally asserting a point of view without undermining the other	A way forward others can relate to	"Sarbanes–Oxley can be a useful tool to examine our governance systems and disciplines"
Illustrating	Helping others to understand through stories	Helps to stimulate conversation, motivation and commitment of others	"Remember our first meeting when we really looked at governance, remember how we reacted?"
Inquiry	Question others and let others question you in order to learn	Aids understanding of the attitudes/ vision that exist in the team	"How did you handle a board of such different personalities and view points?"

Spanning speech forms is both a science and art. The science is the Francis Bacon legacy, that is to be systematic in drawing out the best possible from conversations. The art is to be flexible, adjusting to each person, sitting round the table, each day.

Based on the four speech forms of Habermas, the Boardroom Dynamics Observation Tool captures ways of talking in the boardroom and their effect. When a particular behavior/speech form is observed, tick the appropriate box. Positive and negative behaviors in each of the speech forms are included. Space is provided to register the total number of observed behaviors/speech forms for each board member. At the end of the meeting, pool the observation sheets and explore the level of satisfaction with the meeting. Using the systematically gathered data from each group member, explore what requires improvement.

Through effort and attention, accomplishment in the use of speech forms is realized. To reach such a level of accomplishment requires consideration of one factor, that of controlling ego.

"To listen and not be egoistic, that is how I learnt to get on with people, influence them and have them influence you," says Vadim Makhov. Asked what is involved in harnessing ego, Makhov observes: "To be told. Someone did me a great favour once and told me to keep my ego in check."

Focusing on the salient point

Kelly O'Dea acknowledges the skills of influence through speech. He adds one crucial additional factor, that of maintaining focus. "You listen to many contributions as part of a collaborative process, constantly zooming in on the common threads and themes. When you do that well, you are respected for keeping the team on track and moving things forward."

Listening is critical. So, too, is the discipline of attentiveness to the essence of the discussion. "The skill is to, on the one hand, listen but also draw out from the colleagues on the board the salient features of any debate. In that sense, I think you have to have tact," observes Jeremy Pope, Chairman of MilkLink.

Boardroom dynamics observation tool

Tick each time a behavior is observed.

Date			Items Discussed							

Start time: ___ Finish time: ___

Speech Form	Boardroom Behaviors	Chair	CEO	CFO	NED/ OD 1	NED/ OD 2	NED/ OD 3	NED/ OD 4	NED/ OD 5
Framing/reframing Increases one's/others' awareness of shared questions, vision or mission – not assuming that others have the same frame of reference	**Summarizing:** Repeats, clarifies, confirms, explains, and reflects								
	Agreeing: Acceptance, concurrence, or approval								
	Disagreeing: Reasoned difference of views, criticism, or direction of a position or proposal (not personal)								
	Mediating: Arbitrage								
	Operating: Suggesting process, approach, way of operating, or conducting the meeting								
	Proposing: Putting forward, extending/developing proposal, concept, or course of action								
	Expressing: Giving opinion, analysis, assessment, evaluation, point of view								
Advocating Clarifies the way forward – explicit assertion without reference to other person(s) context	**Informing:** Providing or presenting information, answers, facts, context, or background date								
	Confronting: Antagonistic, autocratic, hostile, obstructive, or personal criticism								
	Colluding: Suspicion that agreement/undertaking have been reached prior to the meeting concerning (non)inclusion of agenda items, position of agenda items, ordering items								

Continued

Continued

Speech Form	Boardroom Behaviors	Chair	CEO	CFO	NED/ OD 1	NED/ OD 2	NED/ OD 3	NED/ OD 4	NED/ OD 5
Illustrating Helps stimulate commitment/ motivation to the way forward – helping others understand through stories	**Relating:** Experience to situation								
	Storytelling: Using metaphors, analogues, and stories that provide similar or different examples								
	Preparing: Providing insightful information and helping articulate clarity or a perspective for inquiry								
Inquiring Helps to understand the reality of what exists so that one can meaningfully proceed – involves questioning others, in order to learn	**Asking/Seeking:** Soliciting information, clarification, or confirmation of facts, figures, or circumstances								
	Engaging: Inclusive open behavior building trust, positive humor, and raising others' status or showing appreciation								
	Challenging: Critical questioning and evaluation, checking out reliability of assumptions, and justification for actions								
General Tone	**Dispassionate:** Procedural, rational, contorting agenda/ issues focus								
	Positive emotionality: Enthusiastic, exhilarating, overpowering								
	Negative Emotionality: Temperamental, angry, cynical, overbearing, bullying, abusive								
Total Contribution									

Note: NED: nonexecutive director; OD: outside director.

Jeremy Pope contends that the discipline to maintain focus requires use of the softer people skills. Cutting people off or inhibiting expression of their views minimizes their contribution and also shows disrespect. The key is to encourage comment but maintain focus on the topic at hand. It is important to encourage and involve others and summarize. The primary skills of chairing meetings need to be grounded in the reality of knowing the organization.

Ronnie Kells, Chairman, United Drug, Ireland agrees. "I take a particular interest in talking to the managers a couple of levels below. I would do it two ways, walking around the business as I do every time I come here and I also visit one or two parts of the business, get to know the people and understand what the issues are."

The final touch to serious and focused discourse is humor. Through it, difficult messages are made more palatable. "I believe you need an element of good humour to go with it. Although I believe some people are natural born leaders, it is something that you need to learn," says Jeremy Pope.

Thinking several meetings ahead

"It's your job to think meetings ahead. Reorganize what can be achieved today. Then think how long it will take to get full closure. It's partly to do with knowing the people on the board. It's partly to do with being realistic about changing their thinking of the others in the organization," says Tom Sawyer.

Understand those deeply held sentiments, surface them, explore and discuss, focus on the salient points, and one further consideration, realistically recognize the time it takes to mold mindsets. As Tom Sawyer emphasizes, being realistic about what can be achieved means knowing each of the members of the board. Intimacy of understanding of the other is not just about gauging their reactions but about appreciating their style of learning.

Some learn through concepts. They are quick. Give them an idea and the benefits or disadvantages are quickly assessed and a conclusion reached. Such individuals are analytical in the way they structure their argument.

Others learn through experience. Pragmatically inclined, such an individual needs to touch and feel the situation. Little learning takes place until the individual has immersed themselves into the project. However, more down to earth learning takes time in order to fully appreciate the nature of the challenges being faced. People who learn from experience may pride themselves that they are strategic and future-thinking oriented, but in reality they are not. Until a situation hits them in the face they do not fully appreciate what they face.

Still others learn from their interactions with people. Ambience; depth of relationship; warmth of conversation: these are all important ingredients for the learning process. For those analytically inclined, such learning is regarded as too emotional. In contrast, for those that thrive on relationships, analytically driven judgment devoid of immersion in context is too cold, unfeeling, and possibly out of touch. How can a meaningful decision be reached if there is little appreciation of how management, staff, and other stakeholders feel and will react? Without others owning decisions, no progress is made. For the feelings-oriented learner, sterile board meetings lapse into debating societies – endless chatter, no substance.

There still remains a fourth group. A relatively small minority of people learn through pain. Tell them; show them; confront them; and still nothing goes in. Not until that person is hurt and experiences the trauma of not changing, little happens. The question remains, how much pain and for how long does the individual resist before they learn?

Thus, thinking meetings ahead is as much about the positioning of issues as it is about assessing the response of others. Appreciating colleagues' styles of learning and the level of incubation required before an idea hatches requires an awareness of the timescales involved.

What matters is that the chairman recognizes his and others' style of learning and does not unthinkingly assume that his/her approach is that of others. "I read others as they are, not how I would like them to be," concludes James Parkel.

Not the darker side

Positioning ideas so that others become more receptive, using personal charm in order to influence, and thinking meetings and situations ahead are the elements of influencing for favorable outcomes. For the less than accomplished player, adopting the very same tactics comes over as manipulative and overly political. Influencing in order to achieve particular outcomes in diverse and complex circumstances requires thought, sensitivity, and sincerity. Conscious of the reactions of others and adjusting style and approach in order to accommodate contracting personalities is fundamental to the process of influence. Such effort is undertaken in order to emerge with improvements for the board, the management, and the organization.

Influence pursued for personal ends is the darker side. Political maneuvering produces short-term results. All looks well on the surface but not underneath. Sincerely influencing for the betterment of all requires delving deep. The skills in having senior managers and board members declare their values, the position they have adopted, their attitudes and views, are considerable. Sincerity of intent and robustness of conversation are fundamental for board members who work their way through complexity.

Politics is the darker side. Influencing to attain outcomes for the betterment of all is a basic of chairmanship.

Key points

- A high-performing chairman knows what outcomes he or she wishes to achieve at and between board meetings. Influencing to achieve desired outcomes is a prime requirement of chairmanship.
- The first step is to surface the sentiments, views, and concerns that each director may hold but not declare. Undeclared feelings concerning events, circumstances,

$\rightarrow$

and individuals can seriously undermine quality of discussion and commitment to decisions reached.

- The second step draws on the personal strength to discuss and work through underlying tensions. Inhibition to raise uncomfortable issues is shown by research as normal, with approximately 66 percent of top managers not facing up to the unpleasantness of unwelcome conversation.
- The third step involves influencing others to achieve one's desired outcomes. Distinction has been drawn between dialogue and debate (see our discussion in Discipline 3). Dialogue, the ability to view all aspects of the argument and, jointly with other parties, emerge with the best possible decision for the parties concerned, is enabled through dialectics or immersion in the opposite argument in order to gain full understanding. To facilitate improved boardroom dialogue, use is made of Habermas' four speech forms as the vehicle to full exploration and building of commitment to decisions reached. The Boardroom dynamics observation tool offers board members feedback on the efficiency and effectiveness of their conversational form.
- The fourth step focuses on the salient points in boardroom conversation. Intensity of conversation can take discussion in varying and, at times, unproductive directions. Recognizing the salient point and returning board colleagues to that focal point distinctly enhances the productivity of the meeting.
- The fifth step is to think and plan meetings ahead. Doing so requires judging the reactions of board members to the issues under scrutiny and assessing their capacity to respond positively. Recognizing the learning styles of each board member assists the chairman to appreciate the time required for an idea to become accepted.
- The ethics and values of each player determine whether influencing for desired outcomes is used to positive effect or as unwelcome political manoeuver.

Living the values

> Whatever the structure, ultimately, it's down to the quality of the people. You can build in all the checks and balances but it finally comes down to a relationship of trust between all board members.
>
> Lord Clive Hollick, Partner,
> Kohlberg Kravis Roberts & Co;
> Chairman, SBS Broadcasting

"The moral character of the top person is the key," says Bernard Rethore. "The fact is they have to signal these virtues every day. What they stand for is what the organization stands for and that is how they should live."

From Phoenix, Arizona to Sydney, Australia, via London and Moscow, two words were repeated time and time again in the research by the authors of this book: trust and integrity.

Trust is the essence of relationships at the level of top management and between management and the rest of the organization, with shareholders and with other stakeholders. "As a Russian, chairing businesses in the US, Italy and France, so much is down to the trust placed in me as a person and of my business ability, "says Vadim Makhov. "I hope I am seen as a person of integrity."

As the ultimate steward of the organization, the chairman lives trust and integrity on behalf of the organization. Discipline 5 of leading the board is living the values.

This is especially important during times of change and transformation. "The general rule of representing and being an ambassador for the company remains very important," says Terry Burns, chairman of Abbey National. "The job of making sure you've got a balanced board and a notion of succession so that you are combining freshness with continuity, remains."

Abbey National was bought by the Spanish Bank Santander in 2004 for £9.5 billion and is considered as key to the growth of the Spanish parent in financial markets and business banking.[1]

"The purchase has for the first time given Santander a foothold in one of the world's largest financial centres," notes Burns. "The financial markets business could be used as a manufacturing centre to develop products that can be sold throughout the group."

With such ambitions, the role of the board and the skills, prominence, and virtues of the chairman are fundamental to realizing growth. The challenge is to capitalize on the total group's assets, while continuing to remain soundly networked in the home market. Living the values that promote trust will be fundamental to the level of integration needed in the extended Santander group.

Employees, management, the media, and other stakeholders are deeply aware of the real values and ethical stance of the board and CEO. They may not be that aware of the espoused values of the organization. What counts is behavior, the living of the values, irrespective of what is spoken or written down.

Attention then turns to the ethical dilemmas and personal vulnerabilities facing board members and senior management alike. The various philosophical positions that any director can adopt are also important, highlighting the nature of the pulls and pushes each person will face. Nothing and no one is perfect, of course. But the research by the authors of this book confirms that top management and board members face dilemmas. Their responses to those dilemmas crucially affect the reputation and standing of the organization.

So, what is covered in this chapter?

- the fact that actions speak louder than words;
- the criticality of trust;
- knowing one's ethical orientation is fundamental to finding ways through ethical dilemmas;

- knowing the organization and its inconsistencies is an important step to genuinely promoting transparency and ethical behavior across the enterprise;
- knowing yourself is primary to living the values of the organization.

Actions speak louder

Many organizations draft value statements capturing the essence of what the organization stands for, its prime purpose, and the behavior expected from its employees and management. Mission and value statements offer a twofold function: those of providing direction and of clarifying moral standing. For others, the virtues and desired behaviors are implicitly understood but not formally captured.

In order to capture what key messages register with employees and management, we asked senior, middle, and lower level managers, of a cross section of organizations and industries, what in their own terms are the organization's mission, corporate objectives, functional or operating objectives, and key areas of responsibility of the top manager(s) of their enterprise. In terms of top manager responsibilities, as an example, the chairman of the company may have made public statements concerning the corporate responsibilities of the company, and, in so doing, initiated a program of activities to pursue. The CEO, equally, may have outlined growth ambitions through merger and acquisition, or may champion certain operational improvements to customer service or quality standards.[2]

The managers of Swedish and US companies as well as Hong Kong commercial operations emerge as the most knowledgeable and understanding of the mission and values of the organization (Table 5.1). British, French, and German managers report that they hold the lowest level of knowledge of the mission and values of their organization. It should be emphasized, however, that the lowest reported level was 62 percent; at most, two-thirds of British managers hold a shared understanding of their organization's mission and values. German, Hong Kong-based, Swedish, and British managers hold a high level of shared understanding

Table 5.1　What counts? Knowing or believing the mission and goals[a]

	Mission	Corporate goals	Functional goals	Personal responsibilities
Sweden	H	H	M	H
Austria	M	M	M	H
Spain	M	L	M	M
Germany	L	H	M	H
France	L	M	M	H
Britain	L	M	M	H
China	M	M	M	H
Hong Kong	H	H	H	H
United States	H	M	M	H

Note:

Awareness: H – High; M – Medium; L – Low.

[a] For further information on how messages are transmitted in the organization, read A. Kakabadse and N. Kakabadse (1999), *Essence of Leadership*, London, International Thomson, chapters 5 and 8, particularly p. 328.

of the corporate objectives of their organization. The same can be applied to Hong Kong-based managers concerning functional and operating objectives.

The higher ranging scores are clustered around the key and critical areas of responsibility that the chairman and/or CEO have declared as a priority. Personalizing the message invokes greatest attention. Employees and management look to the chairman and CEO to communicate direction through living the message and the values.

The personal touch counts for a great deal. Yet, the more personal the touch, the more trust comes into play. In the same survey, the question of trust was explored. People were asked: who are the top managers in your organization? The chairman, CEO, and corporate center directors, irrespective of whether they held a line or support role as well, were clustered together by the rest of the employees and management. These individuals were the better-known board members and were identified with leading the organization and driving through strategy. Those holding more general management (GM) responsibilities, such as country head, were not seen as top management but as one level below, but nevertheless having a powerful influence on implementation of strategy. Both groups were asked to answer

Table 5.2 Trust at the top (as a percentage of 100)

	Japan		United Kingdom		France		Ireland		Germany		Sweden		Spain		Austria		Hong Kong		United States	
	Top	GM	Top	GM	Top	GM	Top	GM	Top	GM	Top	GM	Top	GM	Top	GM	Top	GM	Top	GM
Trust each other	73		65		66		61		75		71		58		63		71		63	
Not trust each other		61		68		48		67		69		66		51		57		72		51

Note: GM: General management.

one simple, but profound, question: do members of the board/ top team trust each other?

The picture that emerges, captured in Table 5.2, highlights contrasting perspectives on trust.[3] Most top managers across the world agree that as members of the top team (the executive) and of the board the levels of trust between them and their GMs is high. The GMs paint a very different picture: the majority, over 50 percent, states that top team and board members do not trust each other or even their own GMs. In fact, British, Irish, and Hong Kong-based GMs score higher on no trust existing than their bosses score on trust.

Our research suggests that for over two-thirds of the companies trust is an issue requiring attention. This merely adds to the results of a great deal of other research that affirms that the values and responsibilities of the organization or its operational and strategic objectives are clearly heard when championed by the leader. Personalizing the message stimulates others. The downside is losing trust in the leader, which also creates cynicism toward the organization's objectives. Remember Enron.

Trust, truth, and Enron

"Just what the hell is this Enron case all about? Enron just took off balance sheet accounting one step more than most. Stop that, and the whole of investment banking collapses!"[4]

These are the words of an Australian senior investment banker transfixed by the case of Enron. In his view, most corporations are Enrons but by another name.

What is interesting is that the late Kenneth Lay, Enron's former chairman, and Jeffrey Skilling, former CEO, both denied they did anything wrong. Other Enron employees representing investor relations, accounts, and general counsel concerned with Lay and Skilling also claimed they were innocent but it is reported that in order to secure lighter sentences they pleaded guilty on lesser charges and agreed to act as prosecution witnesses.

The prosecution argued that Lay and Skilling misled the markets, Wall Street, investors, and even their own employees and management concerning the financial health of the organization. In particular, Sherron Watkins, labeled as the Enron whistle-blower, drew attention not only to irregularities of accounting but also to suspect governance in that the legal firm charged with investing "accounting irregularities" was an inappropriate choice due to the fact that they had approved previous transactions.

The outcome most know: Lay and Skilling were found guilty, still protesting their innocence. It is amazing how many in the investment banking industry still question just what the problem was with Enron. If the whistle-blowing had not captured such public attention, confidence in the company may not have been lost and the firm would be alive and kicking today; that at least is one opinion held in the investment banking industry.

The undisclosed reality is that it could so easily have been many others. At a private dinner, one chairman admitted: "By the grace of God, that could have been me. I am not a crook but the company and all those who depend on it would suffer if I did not do business the way the market expects." In many cases of corporate wrongdoing what emerges is just the tip of an iceberg. Under the surface, so-called wrongdoing was, at the time, an acceptable way of working.

Questions about ethics, morality, behavior, and virtue are of increasing interest to the media and government and virtually always lead to the same conclusion – managers should behave in the right manner. The should imperative is forceful but, unfortunately, life is not so simple. Clearly distinguishing right and wrong acts as a guide but does not account for real life. Despite all the advice and ethical training, scandals have arisen and will continue to arise, with the majority of those enmeshed vehemently protesting their innocence.

The overwhelming majority of the people holding senior office are not crooks but upright and moral citizens. "In all my years, I have encountered few who do not uphold the highest ethical standards," says Bernard Rethore.

Why, then, do these seemingly virtuous people not always do the right thing? Philosophers would say that it is because of the nature of leadership. Leaders face dilemmas that the rest of us do not. They are held to account in ways that most other people are not.

The notion of right, wrong, what is ethical, or unethical is derived from our sense of morality. But in reality, ethics is a term of philosophy, not morality, and is derived from the Greek *ethikos* and *ethos*, meaning custom or usage. The original term meant common practice. For Aristotle, slavishly following so-called right actions achieves little. People need to think for themselves what choices need to be made. Strength of character, personal standards, commitment, and reflection are predeterminates for resolving dilemmas. Aristotle, like Socrates, disliked morality pushed down one's throat. The individual determines his or her own ethical platform to act as the guide for the resolving of dilemmas.

Ethics and morality hold certain parallels in meaning. Both are concerned with appropriate conduct, rules, and outcomes. Both terms can be used to denote appropriate conduct at the personal, team, departmental, and total corporate level. Further, a multitude of ethical moralities exist. Each has its own distinctions. Each has certain similarities. The Confucian "do unto others as they should do to you" holds a remarkable parallel with the Christian "an eye for an eye and a tooth for a tooth." The New Testament version of Christ's moral philosophy of forgiveness is virtually identical to the Jewish golden rule of "what is hateful to you do not do to your neighbour."

Morality and ethics have also become intertwined with social norms. Most Indo-Christian cultures, for example, have a preoccupation with time – be on time, do not be late, keep to the deadline. To break time commitments can be seen on a scale from rude to unethical. Other cultures struggle to understand what all this rigidity about time is about. Social relationships and their continuous bonding is much more important. Therefore, in thinking about moral standards and ethical behaviors, certain fundamentals have to be considered hand in hand with social expectations in order to emerge with a sense of acceptable virtue and personal standards of moral worth.

In reality, people's choices are determined by logic – deduction and rational thinking – as well as their emotions – how they feel about the circumstances they are in. These two simple terms, thinking and feeling, have acted as the basis for the most powerful philosophical platforms from ancient time to today: *teleology*, that of being driven by what others think and thus emotionally adhering to context and *deontology*, logically deducing what is right and to hell with what you think of me.

What you think of me

The philosophy of teleology has its roots in ancient Greece. What is good or bad is examined from the perspective of consequences. According to teleology, the actions of a person can only be considered as ethical or unethical when their impact on a situation is evident. Teleology assumes contextual sensitivity which, in turn, not only enables the individual to understand what is happening around them but also that very same understanding limits their ability to act.

"If you think badly of me, I will not do it."

Yet the converse is also true. If everyone else is doing it, then it is okay for me to do it, just like the banker who wondered what the fuss was about Enron.

Over time, the philosophy of being driven by consequences divided into two camps: egoism and utilitarianism. Egoism focuses on the individual and their interests. Thus, the philosophical stance of egoism is that acting against one's personal interests is contrary to reason. 'First, what's in it for me? Then we can talk about what's in it for us."

Egoism as a philosophy is captured by the economist Adam Smith, in his *The Wealth of Nations.*[5] Smith purported that the only way to achieve the common good is by the individual first promoting their good and well-being. Thus, it is rational and ethical to promote and improve one's own interests. For Adam Smith, certain conventional moralities are tinged with irrational sentiments for the individual's attention is diverted to first thinking of community. Egoism is powerful. Nothing happens until the person is ready and first attending to their interests. In many ways, the United States, as a nation, has adopted Adam Smith and consequentialist egoism. The holding sacred of the rights of the individual customer and consumer and the satisfaction of the person have been central to the American way of thinking. The individual is placed on a pedestal. The great hero – the one man or woman – you can make a difference are powerful messages. The upside is that the motivated person drives others forward to the benefit of all. The downside is that once satisfied the rest of the world is ignored. So with egoism, accompanying the striving for achievement is an inherent selfishness. Further, egoism does not offer ways to resolve conflicts between interests other than through the use of brute force. The strongest wins.

As egoism focuses on the consequences for me, utilitarianism, in contrast, takes a communitarian view. The consequences of actions on the community or society at large are the central consideration. Account has to be taken of the greatest good for the greatest number or at least the fewest negative consequences for others. Utilitarianism proposes that the leader should balance the consequences of their actions and weigh these against alternatives, concluding what is in the community's best interests.

What is in the best interests of the organization and how can the most upbeat, optimistic message be portrayed? How many times has such a thought gone through the mind of a chairman and, or, CEO? Kenneth Lay took that line as part of his defense. The question is when does optimism tip over into illegality?

Utilitarianism was championed by two outstanding philosophers, Jeremy Bentham and John Stuart Mill.[6] Unlike Adam Smith, they place more emphasis on the effect of an individual on the broader array of stakeholders. The irony is that Bentham, a communitarian, demanded that on his death, his body be preserved and placed in a public place for all to see. To this day, close to the entrance to University College, London, Bentham's body, perfectly preserved, is seated and visible for all to view in the entrance corridor leading into the College.

The upside to utilitarianism is the constant thinking of others. The downside is ultimately anything goes. As long as everyone else does likewise. On this basis, human sacrifice would continue today in that the pain of one or a small minority is acceptable as long as the majority feel themselves closer to the God of their choosing. The prime argument against utilitarianism is that certain actions are simply wrong and cannot be justified on the pretext of happiness for the majority. The more serious critique leveled against utilitarianism is how best choice can be made if the individual and the community do not have a sound, moral platform to begin with? The accusation is that utilitarianism ignores actions that are wrong as long as the ends justify the means. Consequentialist philosophy has the potential to violate society's basic sense of justice.

Who cares what you think of me!

The contrast to teleology is the philosophy of deontology, of being driven by an inherent sense of what is right. Duty is to doing what is good and right, irrespective of the consequences. Action should not be justified by its consequences on individuals and communities but by its inherent rightness. Deontology promotes moral sense and strength of character. Ends do not justify means. Preserving individual rights and conforming to moral principles lies at the heart of deontological philosophy.

The German philosopher, Emmanuel Kant promulgated a deontological theory of ethics.[7] According to Kant, there exist certain universal principles which stand above the concerns of circumstance and person, and because of their absolute virtue, need to be paid homage.

Respecting people's rights, promoting justice in society, and working toward a universal good for all are admirable as aspirations as well as actions. However, the downside is who can constantly behave to such high standards? How can overriding moral principles driven by one single reason fit all? What does an individual do in circumstance of conflicting duties and loyalties? What do you do when two different individuals or groups both have justifiable rights but those rights are in conflict with each other? For example, the right to have access to information through the Freedom of Information legislation may, in turn, undermine the privacy rights of persons and corporations.

Without a way forward through such dilemma, individuals are vulnerable to being manipulated or committing unlawful acts simply because of one overriding but uncompromising principle being pushed down everyone's throat. Those more pragmatic in the sense of being conscious of the consequences of their action are unlikely to blindly accept duty without questioning.

Right and wrong

We are not suggesting that teleology and deontology should be placed on the agenda of the next board meeting. But the issues they raise are important – and increasingly so.

In their description of their chairman, the CEO, the president, the board members, and the senior managers from different parts of the world adopted a variety of terms to denote moral standing and ethical worth. In similar vein, so too did chairmen in describing themselves and other chairmen they have known.

The use of deontological language, *moral, worthy, ethical*, and phrases, *uncompromising in making the difficult but ethically right choice*, is common particularly among US chairmen and top directors, less so among others.

To display and live to the highest of moral standards is not just a precondition of holding senior office but also a requirement of ever greater corporate governance demands. Whether through stock exchange listing or legislation, particular standards are set and the organization and its directors judged accordingly.

No matter where in the world, the board and senior management set the tone of the organization. The leaders of the organization promote, intentionally or unintentionally, the ethical standards of the enterprise. Yet, each organization and circumstance will pose a new and different challenge to what has been experienced. Even the leader with strong convictions is likely to be challenged as contexts are dynamic, ever changing. To try and be consistent in duty is probably impossible. Thus, acting responsibly and ethically demands reflection about one's own personal convictions as well as the reality of circumstances.

Also, simply understanding the depth of resilience required to face up to challenges is an additional consideration. No matter how clever or good the person, holding senior office means facing dilemmas.

In better appreciating one's ethical self, the following statements examine a person's ethical nature. Before answering, the following statements need to be given deep consideration. One should reflect on one's role as board member, chairman, independent director, CEO, or member of the top team, and how one behaves and addresses the challenges one faces. One should be honest with oneself. Once it is felt that one has a realistic view of one's attitudes, thoughts, and actions, then one can respond by ticking the appropriate box next to each statement.

Checklist of the ethical self: What you really stand for

	Column 1	Column 2
1. I consistently apply the same principles to all	Y	N
2. In reality, I more consider what is the greatest good for the greatest number	N	Y
3. I religiously apply governance principles through the organization	Y	N
4. I recognize I need to be flexible with making governance work in the organization	N	Y
5. I consider what is best for me before I proceed	N	Y
6. I always prioritize my duties before my personal interests	Y	N
7. I act in ways which are in my/my circle's best interest but judge others according to their duty	N	Y
8. I reach understandings with important others	N	Y
9. I have no understandings with others but live by clear values and behaviors	Y	N
10. I judge others the way I judge myself	Y	N
11. Winning hearts and minds means being flexible	N	Y
12. For consistency, I document and circulate the values and standards of behavior expected in the organization	Y	N
13. I really do not care what others think of me	Y	N

Continued

Continued

	Column 1	Column 2
14. I do care what people important to me think of me	N	Y
15. I always make the difficult decision	Y	N
16. Even involving someone close to me, I still make the difficult decision	Y	N
17. I recognize and accept my inconsistencies	N	Y
18. I recognize my inconsistencies and always put that right	Y	N
19. I know when to turn a blind eye	N	Y
20. I never turn a blind eye	Y	N
21. I would ignore a minor unethical act	N	Y
22. Even with minor transgressions, I take action	Y	N
23. I balance acting on transgressions against guarding the reputation of the organization	N	Y
24. I act on any wrongdoing irrespective of the outcome	Y	N
25. Whatever is written down, I tell those around me, "Look, this is the way business is really done!"	N	Y
26. I define what ethics means to this organization and live by that	Y	N
27. I know what should be done, don't always do it, but feel guilty afterwards	N	Y

Note:

Y – Yes; N – No.

If all or most of your responses appear in Column 1, then your ethical inclination is deontological. You are a man or woman of principle, but can be – or appear to be – rigid, uncompromising, and cold.

If all or most of your responses appear in Column 2, then your ethical inclination is teleological. You are flexible, responsive to the needs of others, probably liked by many, a networker, and viewed as caring and warm. However, you are also likely to be viewed as inconsistent. Particularly under pressure, you are more likely to favor friends and your immediate circle and do not always keep to your promises.

As there are 27 questions, you cannot emerge as well balanced. However, if your responses per column are almost equal, whatever the outcome, you are teleological but you kid yourself that you are a man or woman of principle. So:

- If you emerge as deontological, you are likely to be respected.
- If you emerge as teleological, you are likely to be liked.
- If you emerge with relatively well-balanced scores, probably most do not trust you but few dare tell you that.

Working through the above checklist not only helps identify the messages each individual projects but also their level of maturity and resilience to face up to uncomfortable challenges. Experience suggests that most others see us in our true light, especially if those others hold a subordinate position. Their future and sometimes survival depends on them accurately judging the boss's psychological, behavioral, and ethical profile. The most mistrusted director is the one who has a misleading or inaccurate view of themselves. The worst director is the one who is deontological to others but teleological about themselves. That director more likely ends up with a siege mentality, not understanding why they are both disliked and disrespected.

Leaders, simply by the breadth of discretion in their role (see Discipline 1), display their deeper and more intimate self daily. That is life. In so doing, the true corporate and social responsibilities of leaders are exhibited, not by their spoken or written words, but by their actions. Respecting any leader requires identifying with the ethical message(s) the leader lives by. Consistency is key.

Being consistently teleological is being seen as a warm and likeable rogue. If you are on my side, you will benefit.

Being consistently deontological is being respected, possibly feared, but viewed as fair and having no favorites. Do your job. Respect the guidelines and standards set and you will be judged accordingly. Liked or disliked, each one is rewarded according to their merit and performance.

What you are like as the chairman profoundly influences others.

Responsibility of the corporation

Now we turn from the ethics of the individual to those of the corporation.

"We are a power company. Of course we have a broad range of responsibilities, not just to our employees and shareholders, but to the communities that we serve. Safety is however the critical number one agenda item," observes Sir John Parker, chairman of National Grid.

John Parker's comments on responsibility extending beyond the boundaries of the organization to a broader group of stakeholders fall squarely into the arena of corporate social responsibility (CSR). CSR refers to the broader responsibilities of the firm, attentive to the needs of a broad spectrum of stakeholders.

CSR is an emotive issue. "I am sick and tired of the CSR hype. At best it is just words; at worst it is a mechanism for sucking profit out of the business," comments one director of an international company. "We say all the right things, but in reality it means nothing. CSR for us is a trumped up form of PR and what else would it be?" adds an American director. The American director says:

> How can our company, constantly striving to battle with costs so that our shareholders stay off our backs, then go and spend on CSR? Other than sponsoring gimmicks which capture favourable attention from the press and media, anything else and the shareholders will ask questions. For me, CSR is GAR – government absolving their responsibility.

For many, CSR is little more than window dressing. "I suspect that you will find tobacco companies and armaments companies invest more in CSR than anyone else," a skeptic told us.

CSR is a contentious issue and the spread of the debate is enormous, ranging from the view that corporate responsibility lies in the fabric of the organization to the consideration of responsible use of shareholder funds to those who consider CSR as hype of the political correctness variety. Many view CSR as a passing phase.

Others are not so sure. "CSR is hardly mentioned in the States but we expect that to change. Just look at the world; it's obvious CSR is here to stay," says Ellen Van Velsor of the Center for Creative Leadership. "And businesses everywhere are learning how to handle it." Evidence supports Ellen Van Velsor. CSR is here to stay. It is now a topic that the corporation cannot ignore.

But, despite its increasing prominence, the challenge remains: with whom does social responsibility really lie? Is CSR the unnecessary spend of shareholder funds? Is there common agreement concerning the core meaning of the term?

When chairman of Pearson, the publisher, and currently of HBOS, the UK-based international bank, Dennis Stevenson has positioned CSR investment in line with the business of both organizations. Stevenson says:

> At Pearson, we spend 99 percent of our money in the community on educational projects. In HBOS, we reined it all in and our monies are spent largely on financial literacy and also on projects which involve members of our employees volunteering. Narrowly defined so as to get better value for the community (and the company) for the money we spend.

The debate is ongoing and can be usefully traced back to Adam Smith's, *The Wealth of Nations*. Smith placed free market economics as a form of moral philosophy. Since his writings of the 1760s, many have taken up that calling. Milton Friedman championed what is known as the neoclassical position by stating that the ultimate social responsibility of business, if pursued in an ethical manner and in obedience to the law, is business. Thus, one form of CSR is the neoclassical shareholder model.

Another form of CSR emerged in 1953 with the American writer, Howard Bowen, who outlined the social responsibilities of business.[8] Scholars latched on, driven by their growing concern for the discrepancies between wealth creation and the socioeconomic reality of its distribution. The United States, probably more than any other nation, has been accused of rampant consumerism and, as a result, immoral business practice. From Bowen's book rose the movement of the firm serving society beyond that of obligation to shareholders. The CSR case is not entirely the dream of idealists. The Introduction chapter of this book refers to the long history of social concern, evident in both the United States and Continental Europe, championed by Christian values-driven entrepreneurs. Providing decent wages and other social and material benefits has gone hand in hand with the promotion of one or other aspect of Christianity. As shown, homes built close to the factory out of concern for employee welfare were done so by other owner managers for ease of control, productivity, and effective cost management. Thus, although placed on the map by Howard Bowen, corporate philanthropy has a solid 160-year history.

There is still a third interpretation of CSR. The social reformist movements pre– and particularly post–World War II in Scandinavia have given rise to an expectation of social well-being. Here, government plays a far more active role than is the case with the Anglo-American economies. Taxation is far higher for both the citizen and the corporation. Despite the global prominence of the ethos of shareholder value, to be obviously rich is frowned upon. Social redistribution is deep in the Scandinavian psyche. It is expected that government be attentive to inequalities and new social needs. It is the government that directs resources to these points. Thus, the corporation is a tool of the community.

From social redistribution we move on to the fourth interpretation of CSR, that of environmental sustainability. Partly as a result of a long history and partly due to the influential Brundtland Report, named after the former Danish Head of State, Denmark, France, Germany, and certain other central European nations focus on the ecosphere.[9] Social responsibility is to understand and respond to the needs of a silent stakeholder, the environment.

Contrasting CSR perspectives have stood actively side by side forever twenty years now. From these bases, a myriad of interpretations have arisen capturing the views of academicians, political pressure groups, government, agencies, and corporations.

Even the CSR agencies and pressure groups do not agree on desired CSR outcomes.

Four separate waves of social and corporate responsibility concern have been identified since the 1950s. The late 1950s and 1960s witnessed CSR1, the development of research and thinking on business ethics and corporate social responsiveness. With that as the platform, the mid-1970s witnessed CSR2, an identification of the social duties of the corporation. The debate matured by the mid- 1980s and led to CSR3, commonly termed corporate social rectitude and formed ways of improving business or societal relationships. Discussion of relationship of the corporation with its array of stakeholders led to challenging the free market view of the centrality of the firm. Thus emerged CSR4, a broader dialogue on cosmos, science, and religion, a theme that continues to this day.

CSR covers a very wide span. Yet, despite good intention and considerable intellectual investment, one strongly held view prevails captured by Matthew Bishop, business editor of *The Economist*, who argues that company-sponsored CSR programs are little more than attempts to keep civil pressure at a distance so that business can proceed as normal.[10] There is some support for this view.

Our research indicates that the Continental Europeans are more CSR conscious, the Anglo-Americans less so. "Terms such as CSR and sustainability just make me sick. All I know is that I have to pretend this nonsense," said one US vice president in a manufacturing organization.

The reality is that there is a world of difference between what is stated and implemented. The chasm between words and reality is not unusual. But CSR is now a political issue. Ineffective practice trickles to the press and media. If nothing else, inattention to CSR leaves corporate reputation vulnerable.

Know your organization

So what are the lessons about living the values?

First, know your organization: What terms capture the nature or culture of the organization? Does shared agreement exist on the values and culture of the organization? What are the weaknesses of the organization? What tensions within the organization remain unresolved?

For the chairman, in particular, living the values of the organization requires consciousness of its inconsistencies. The more functional the values, safety, production efficiency, product or service quality, in effect the basics, the fewer the likely inconsistencies between what is stated and reality. The more higher order the values, trust, care about development of people and communities, the more challenging they are to live up to.

Knowing your organization is knowing the inconsistencies or mixed messages that are transmitted daily. Knowing your organization is, transparently, doing something about those inconsistencies.

What are the sources of inconsistency?

- **Senior managers/directors giving one message but doing something different**. The tensions and inconsistencies increase when support is given at key meetings and the very same person with their team or on their home turf instructs that policies and communications from the center should be ignored.
- **Remuneration**. This is a particularly vexed topic. Substantial differences in remuneration can lead to alienation and a feeling of being exploited and hence a lack of identification with the policies of the center. The difference between the pay of the average operative and the average CEO in the following countries is 4589–1400:1, United States;[11] 180–18:1, United Kingdom; 15:1, Japan; 13:1, Germany; and 3:1, Cyprus. Other than Cyprus, where executive remuneration is so far out of step with all the others, the question is for whom and for what do employees and middle management think they work?
- **Economic life cycle**. Particularly for firms that operate a group structure, there is no reason to assume that the various divisions and subsidiaries progress at the same economic pace. Certain subsidiaries may be maturing, reaching the end of their economic life cycle. Their only competitive advantage is price. All depends on the economy of scale disciplines introduced by management. From corporate center's point of view,

the next step is to sell the subsidiary. Yet, within the same portfolio is another subsidiary or division that is exciting, unique, and at the early stage of the economic life cycle. With such diversity of needs within the group of companies, inconsistency of strategy and policy implementation is normal.

- **Charisma**. The style, mannerisms, need for recognition by others and influence on others by certain key managers can grow particular cliques and subcultures. A fast moving sales team headed by a charismatic and loyal sales director, can make a powerful contribution to the organization. An equally influential senior manager may undermine colleagues, not for reasons of differences of vision or strategy but purely through ego. The destructive charismatic leader models divisiveness. It is not too long before negativity becomes ground into the firm.
- **Style of communication**. All managers have their attractive and undesirable idiosyncrasies, both are particularly evident when communicating emotive messages through the organization. Flamboyant sales and marketing directors communicating through formal and informal meetings with their people stand out as heroes when compared against an introverted CEO or finance director who experiences presentations as uncomfortable. Depending on the nature of the message to be delivered, consideration of content and style of communication become ever more important.
- **Legacy**. What is the history of the organization? Who were the culture champions of the past? Did a charismatic senior manager dominate the enterprise for any length of time and leave a legacy against which successors are judged? Similar to Daphne Du Maurier's novel, *Rebecca*, where the new wife is judged against the idealized characteristics of the previous deceased spouse, are the faults of the new leader overemphasized while the shortcomings of the previous leader are conveniently forgotten? Legacy is a powerful force. The symbols of history are evident as soon as one leaves the front door; flags, monuments, pictures of a brave and glorious past adorn schools, shops, streets, and squares. Depending on the sophistication of the organization and its established senior management, breaking with the past can be career threatening.

As chairman, living the values of the organization requires knowing and, at times, openly disclosing its inconsistencies.

Most in the organization will both know and have a view of the enterprise's mixed messages. To deny knowing inconsistency is to not acknowledge the reality of others and, in so doing, distance people from the values and aspirations of top management and the board?

Living the values of the organization requires living the experience of others.

Know yourself

Living the values of the organization also demands knowing yourself.

Our research consistently identifies the qualities critical for the world-class chairman (Table 5.3).

Being trusted and displaying integrity are universally rated as mandatory qualities. Without these the office of chairman is irreparably damaged. The remaining qualities, although important, fall into the "nice to have" category.

Knowing oneself and, by implication, one's own inconsistencies allows for living the key values. Being smart, but not acknowledging the organization's and one's undesired characteristics leads to a leader who is barely tolerated.

Being smart, acknowledging the organization's inconsistencies but not one's own is a leader who is respected but from a distance. Being smart, acknowledging the organization's and one's own inconsistencies and turning them to advantage resembles charismatic leadership. Even being not too smart is forgiven.

Table 5.3 Qualities of the chairman

- Trust
- Integrity
- Patience
- Understanding
- Persistence
- Humility
- Self-reflection
- Ability to act as model for others

The advice can be summarized: be streetwise and just a little bit humble.

Key points

- The chairman, together with the CEO, symbolizes the values of the organization.
- The attitudes and behavior that the chairman and CEO exhibit may or may not represent the true values of the organization but are likely to be seen to do so. In fact, in terms of communication, personal statements by the chairman and CEO are identified as having the more profound effect on others, in and external to the organisation.
- The two fundamental qualities of chairmanship, trust and integrity, emphasize the public face of the chairman and the need to be sensitive to knowing what it means to live the values of the organization.
- Trust in the chairman as a person and also as a representative of the organization is undermined when public statements concerning value-determined or ethical behavior are not matched by behavior.
- Matching words with behavior is distinctly challenging as each individual's personal ethics and the pressure of circumstances may be such that good intentions may be frustrated and the individual does not have the values they proclaim.
- It is commonplace for inconsistencies to exist between declared value statements and behavior due to complexities within the organization and/or due to poor self-awareness on the part of the chairman and CEO.
- In order to live out the values of the organization, it is important to understand one's own ethical orientation. Two ethical platforms have been the center of philosophical debate for many centuries, that of teleology, on being driven by circumstances, and that of deontology, that of being driven by principles and not context.

$\rightarrow$

- In order to further minimize the inconsistency between the words spoken and consequent action, intimately knowing the organization is as important as knowing oneself.
- Clarifying the corporate and social responsibilities of the organization and ensuring that protocols are in place to realize such responsibilities are duties that fall upon the chairman.
- In clarifying the responsibilities of the organization, it is important to recognize that CSR is rapidly becoming a political issue due to the varying interpretations of the term, either by company, public agency, political pressure group, geographic location, or maturity of national economy in terms of CSR adoption.

Developing the board

> The chairman is responsible for the development of the executive board.
>
> Herbert Müller CEO,
> Ernst & Young, Germany

Every year, companies invest huge amounts of time and money on executive development and education. Yet very little is spent on formally developing the board. Instead, board directors are somehow expected to step over the threshold of the boardroom fully formed or to magically transform themselves.

The best chairmen know this is not how it really happens. They recognize the need to develop themselves and their fellow directors, individually and collectively, in order to forge an effective board: developing the board is Discipline 6.

Study clearly shows that developing the board requires the following:

- board assessment and review;
- in-depth profiling of individuals and their dynamics on the board;
- attention to director development;
- attention to the development of the chairman;
- how to pick and use consultants and facilitators well;
- how to manage the transition into the new job.

Board assessment and review

With Sarbanes–Oxley in the United States, increasing CEO turnover, and far greater focus on governance than ever before,

it would appear on the surface at least that the chairman's job
has changed significantly over recent years. Some suggest that
the churn of chairmen is increasing. Not so, says Sir Mark Moody-
Stuart, chairman of Anglo American. "It hasn't changed," he
responds. As Moody-Stuart says:

> The Combined Code in the UK clarified the role of the board
> and the non-executives, but it didn't really change the role.
> Clearly, there's stronger emphasis on governance at the
> moment; much stronger emphasis than there was in the past.
> There has been more formalization of processes – like the
> evaluation of the board, the nomination processes, the com-
> position of the board; the balance between executives and
> non-executives; and so on. Those are really clarifications
> rather than changes. Probably the biggest change, and one of
> the most positive, has been the clarification of board evalu-
> ation. This used to be done – and could quite effectively be
> done – by the chairman. It was the chairman's views. Now
> it's much more of a collective effort. It's a clear process and
> that's very good because it ensures that one gets a real inter-
> action between the chairman and each member of the board.
> Each board member really has an opportunity to comment
> and say what they think about the performance of the board.
> That's been a big positive.

So, how do you go about developing the board? BHP Billiton's
Don Argus emphasizes feedback. This includes an overview of
board processes, assessing the contribution of directors and
capturing each board member's view of how effectively the
board functions. Don Argus hires specialist consultants who
also examine his own contribution and effectiveness. This
approach to board development is informal in style but structured and systematic in its approach. A benchmark for performance assessment is established.

Other chairmen extend the development brief to that of executive management.

Herbert Müller explains that in Germany, the approach to board
development not only includes feedback on individual performance but also extends into the realms of compensation, balanced

scorecard assessment, appointments, dismissal, and transitioning into the role of both executive and supervisory board members.

Others adopt a more informal approach to board development. "The development of the board is a state of mind. You don't do development and then do something else. How the board functions and matures is the responsibility of all those on that board," says James Parkell.

Many agree with Parkell's perspective. Unless the board desires development and is willing to respond positively to formally or informally offered comment on how it can improve, investment in development is wasted.

Certain chairmen and board directors speak of development as a matter of mind-set and choice. We agree wholeheartedly with the first point – the development of the board and its members is almost universally accepted as vital to the future performance of the organization. But we disagree that there is a choice in the matter. That was the past. Development is now a must. And the pressure for board and individual director review, assessment, and development is intensifying.

The Canadian academic, Richard Leblanc, points to a growing array of pressure points requiring investment in board development.[1] Among them are the following:

- **Research**. The Change Partnership (2004) survey on "What makes for a great board chair?," for example, answered with "working continuously to improve board performance;"
- **Shareholder activism**. The California Public Employees Retirement System (CalPERS) emphasizes the need for the assessment of board leadership;
- **Voluntary codes**. The UK's Combined Code recommends the performance assessment of the chairman by the independent directors led by the SID;
- **Financial markets**. The Australian Stock Exchange Principles (2003) recommend "the performance evaluation of individual directors" and that that evaluation be disclosed;
- **Policy**. The Canadian Securities Administrators National Policy 58-201, *Corporate Governance Guidelines*, state that "individual directors should be regularly assessed."

A book from Mercer Delta Consulting, *Building Better Boards*, concurs with Richard Leblanc.[2] In it, David Nadler, chairman of Mercer Consulting, and his two coauthors, identify a variety of approaches to board assessment, through surveys, structured interviews, and focus groups. The structured interviews and focus groups allow board members, individually and collectively, to offer their view of the board's strengths, areas for development, and those needs that require priority attention.

Invaluable feedback concerning tensions and lack of shared mind-set comes from the exercise. Nadler et al. consider formal surveys equally valuable as they provide an empirical benchmark of key aspects of board functioning, the appropriateness of the board agenda, time for discussion, quality of ideas exchange, chairman or board member conduct, encouragement to challenge, and resolution of differences.

Similarly, our research identifies key performance parameters which are captured in our survey-based, board performance assessment instrument.

Board performance assessment

	Scale				
	No				Yes
	1				5
Do board members:					
• Have a shared understanding of each other's role and responsibilities?	1	2	3	4	5
• Hold a shared view on the value and contribution of each other?	1	2	3	4	5
• Hold a shared view of the value and contribution of the board?	1	2	3	4	5
• Receive timely and adequate information in order to review and progress against budget?	1	2	3	4	5
• Receive timely and adequate information in order to satisfactorily make decisions?	1	2	3	4	5
• Regularly review and assess strategic performance against plan?	1	2	3	4	5
• Regularly review and assess operational performance against plan?	1	2	3	4	5
• Consider that board agendas reflect the challenges and needs of the organization?	1	2	3	4	5
• Effectively contribute to strategic and operational discussion?	1	2	3	4	5
• Receive feedback on their performance?	1	2	3	4	5
• Regularly review, update and clearly communicate strategy	1	2	3	4	5

Note:

Replies are graded on a scale of 1 to 5 ranging from "No" to "Yes."

1 2 3 – example of spread of responses.

When we run the survey, we identify the resulting spread of responses per question as highlighted and identify the mean score per dimension. Inevitably that varies with each separate survey. Then the aggregate results are first presented to the chairman so that he or she can prepare for a session with the whole board drawing out the implications of the underlying trends. Coupled with insights gained from confidential interviews with each of the board members, the benefits are:

- improved sharing of concerns over board performance and contribution;
- better understanding of the view(s) and position(s) adopted by each of the board members;
- greater disclosure of board dynamics, the nature and relevance of the agenda, the issues debated, and the contribution of individual members and the board;
- greater shared commitment to improve board and individual member performance.

The power of profiling

The discipline of working through a structured board review assessment process often stimulates the necessary level of conversation to surface and addresses board- and management-related issues. Such a process can be facilitated by third parties. In other organizations, the chairman acts as facilitator, interviewer, and participant. The research by the authors of this book indicates that both approaches are viewed as satisfactory. The success of both depends on the circumstances facing each board, the nature of the issues the board is required to address and, particularly, the style and disposition of the chairman.

Yet, irrespective of internal or external facilitation, the danger with board assessment review is the tick box mentality. At worst, directors go through the motions of board review with little faith in the process, privately holding the view that no progress will be made. They may refrain from responding honestly to interview and structured survey assessment, even though they are fully cognizant of the issues facing the board. Such boards are likely to have a history of unresolved and undisclosed tensions and also a numbing fear factor.

Powerful personalities on the board can create a discomforting atmosphere that inhibits openness of conversation and also contribution from other board members on the more basic responsibilities. In such situations, dysfunctional dynamics are likely. The longer these cumbersome and ultimately self-defeating modes of interaction continue, the more deeply they become part of the fabric of the board. Unearthing the nature of these continuously unproductive ways of working then becomes the challenge facing the board.

Difficult questions must be asked: are unwelcome ways of working due to the mind-set and deeply held aspects of each person's character (loosely termed personality) or due to the culture of the board or both? In previous chapters, we examined the powerful effect of culture and how a way of working can become a habit difficult to break. Here, we examine mind-set and the power of the individual to continue or change ways of working.

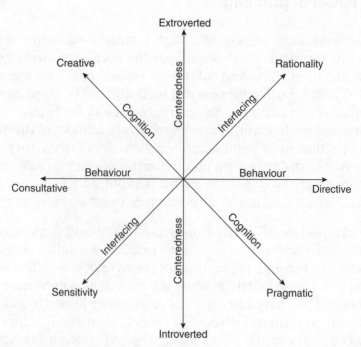

Figure 6.1   Board visioning map

Mind-set

Mind-set refers to ways of thinking, viewing the world, and taking action. How do members of any team, board or not, interpret events and processes and from that consider how to act? Four researchers from the Cranfield School of Management in the United Kingdom, Charles Margerison, Jacquie Drake, Ralph Lewis, and Chel Hibbert, have developed a prototype executive profiling tool that captures certain dimensions of each person's ways of thinking and behavior.

Building on their work, we developed this into a tool we call the visioning map. The visioning map captures how individuals, together with their colleagues, envisage a future and subsequently take action. The map has four dimensions (Figure 6.1).

- **Centeredness** refers to how a person leads their daily life. Some people are more outgoing, taking pleasure, or needing to interact, with a large number of people. The contrast to those who live their life in the outer world, are more introverted individuals, at ease with their own company, living in their inner world, not needing continuous interaction.
- **Behavioral orientation** refers to how individuals behave and whether their way of acting varies by circumstance or is consistent irrespective of the situation. Certain individuals adopt a more directive approach, controlling other people's actions and even ways of thinking. Formal authority or a more command-based style, are used. Others are more consultative, inviting participation and comment on how situations should be handled or concerns addressed. The individual is more team oriented, facilitating a group approach to decision taking and decision implementation and a sharing of responsibility for actions taken and outcomes.
- **Interfacing** examines how individuals relate, interact, and cooperate (or not) across organizational and status boundaries. Certain people are more rational in their approach, attending to the tasks at hand but paying little attention to personal sensitivities and the nuances of context. Their focus is to get the job done with minimal concern for how others feel. The opposite are sensitivity oriented – conscious of others'

concerns and moods. For them interfacing with others is a more personal experience, whereby style and approach need to be adjusted not just according to task demands but also in response to the emotional state of others. Thus, getting on with the task is balanced by feelings. The rationality-oriented board member focuses on the job, even to the point of not knowing that they have upset other people. The more sensitivity-oriented board member focuses on building relationships and may sacrifice the efficiency of getting on with the job for the sake of harmony.

- **Cognition** refers to ways of knowing, forms of knowledge, or ways of instinctively seeing the surrounding world. Certain individuals are intuitive. They grasp the bigger picture. They quickly recognize possibilities. Their imagination and insight, which can be of great advantage when the board faces new and interesting challenges, turns into restlessness or boredom when faced with routine. On the other side, the more pragmatic individual thrives on detail. He or she is practical, relies on experience, and works better with tangible information. Such a person is focused on the here and now and pragmatically works step by step, adopting a steady, even nondramatic, approach to problem solving.

Each individual completes a questionnaire, the results of which are scanned on to the visioning map. For purposes of feedback, each map is placed alongside the other and comment is offered on how each person interprets, challenges, acts, forms relationships, controls or invites participation, and overall how those ways of operating affect the team. How a group gels or not, how the group communicates with each other, how effectively issues are addressed, and the level of commitment to decisions are uncovered.

Preceding the feedback event, confidential one-to-one interviews are undertaken, informing the facilitator of the business issues facing the board and individual opinions of the effect of team dynamics to decision outcomes. Such perceptions are then contrasted with the results emerging from the visioning mapping process. The visioning mapping process not only surfaces the present, but is also sufficiently accurately predictive of board dynamics and decision outcomes for up to 65 months ahead of time, other things being equal. The economists' phrase of other things being equal is particularly pertinent. The purpose of offering intense, penetrating feedback to all members of a board is that other things should not be equal! People change and the process of deep feedback is designed to stimulate change in individuals and, as a result, in the whole group. Even small change along any of the four axes can have a significant impact on individual and group behavior. The strap line is "1 percent change in the individual has a 10 percent improvement on overall board performance." The multiplier effect is powerful.

The ambitious but angry board

To see how the visioning map works in practice, consider the following example. The board of a well-known American IT company debated the expansionist plans of management. The CEO/chairman had a reputation for being aggressive and wanting to be the world's No. 1.

The CEO/Chairman had set his mind on the acquisition of a foreign, prestigious company, which would allow access to newly emergent, but likely lucrative, economies of the future. The CEO tabled the proposition as a merger, admitting it was nothing more than an acquisition. Appreciative of the strategic significance of the target, certain of the other board members were uncomfortable with the price; the target company was overvalued, a point which the CEO acknowledged. His view was, "that's the state of the market today." Should the acquisition be successful, funds for further investment would not be available. Further, the response of the target organization was unwelcoming. If successful, the acquisition would be hostile. One of the directors, seen as different to the others, spoke privately to the CEO/chairman stating that to proceed would end up damaging the parent company. Aside from price, the director's concern was that the parent had not developed the capability for post-merger integration. A high price would be paid – the better managers would walk to competitors eager for their services, leaving a shell of a company.

"Fine, so what do you suggest?" was the retort of the CEO/chairman.

The CEO was persuaded to bring in a consultant with whom he quickly gelled. Each board member was then interviewed by the consultant and feedback given to the CEO/chairman. The news was not good. Internal strife, lack of commitment, hostility, and denial of anything wrong, was the essence of the message. The CEO/chairman wanted the board to be offered the same feedback. The consultant felt that was inappropriate. In private, all would know the findings as accurate. In public, they would blame the consultant for "having got it wrong." The board would be worse off. The consultant suggested participation in the visioning mapping exercise. To his surprise, the CEO/chairman agreed and asked the board to proceed. The board members completed the questionnaires. The results were as follows.

Directive, rational, with an amazing eye for detail surpassed only by his memory for commitments made, decisions taken and then how well they are followed through, the CEO/chairman listened, but only up to a point. He is person No. 1 – see Figure 6.2. His attention span to consultation was minimal. Once he heard enough and he knew what steps to take, he listened no more. Person No. 2 is one of the external independent directors,

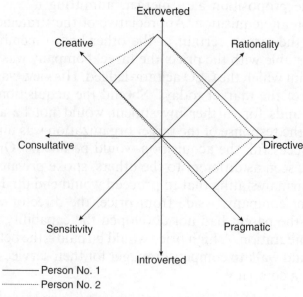

Figure 6.2   Drive it through

similar in profile to the CEO/chairman with a marginally greater grasp of possibilities but less attention to detail. Both listen little. Once the mind of both is made up, nothing will shake them. The two individuals were personal friends and the friendship was evident to the others on the board. However, some of the other board members considered that should the two disagree that would end their collegiality. The two dominated board meetings.

Not as extroverted and gregarious were three other board members, similarly directive, similarly quick to judge and listen up to a point, less intuitively smart to recognize and grasp opportunities, but much more personally sensitive (Figure 6.3). Their introverted nature made them appear quiet and cooperative. Underneath, these three were seething. They perceived the CEO/chairman as a bully and together with what the three termed as his alter ego external independent director, owned everything they proposed. The three were switched off and

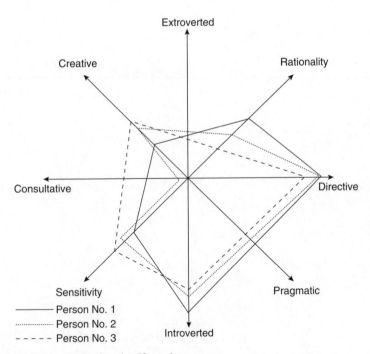

Figure 6.3 Switched off and angry

angry, not necessarily disagreeing with the CEO/chairman, but despising his approach and demeanor.

That was not always the case. When the three were being recruited on to the board, the CEO/chairman was viewed as charismatic – a leader, the man who would take the organization to glory. Not any longer. Feeling powerless to challenge; seemingly unable to muster the speed of mind to offer alternative perspectives, the three had reduced their contribution to posing questions and intervening on points of detail. Most board meetings they sat in sullen silence.

Unusual for an American centric board was the chief financial officer (CFO); he sat as a full board member (Figure 6.4). The other members of the management team only attended board meetings when invited. All acknowledged that the CFO was the most intellectually sharp of that group. He had a capacity to switch from one topic to the next, draw linkages and themes together, where others had not seen any relationship and, unusually

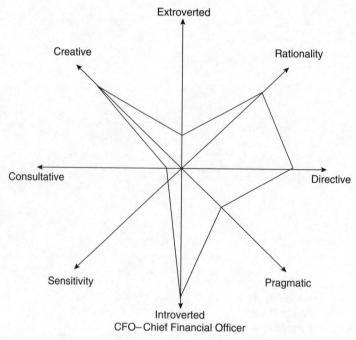

Figure 6.4   CFO as CEO

for someone so mentally quick, had a sharp eye for detail. Most people that are so intuitive become bored when faced with undue routine. Not the CFO; he persevered. In fact, he persevered to such an extent that he not only out-thought the CEO/chairman but also argued his corner endlessly until he won the day – by wearing down the opposition. Even the CEO/chairman found him a handful and resented giving ground to someone who was "more right" than him.

Unaware of the impact he had on others, the CFO was viewed as cold, uncompromising, ruthless, and secretive. He listened as little as his other board colleagues but he was open about that – "What do I need to listen to? I am already there and ahead," was one of his favored retorts. His colleagues admiring of his many skills but fearful of appearing to look foolish should they challenge him, excused his rampant disregard of others by stating "he's an investment banker. What do you expect? Everything is a quick fix and deal." There was some truth in the comment as the CFO had minimal managerial and board experience and as the protégé of the CEO/chairman was catapulted to his current managerial and board director roles as a result of his intellect and deal track record.

One person stood out on the board as different from the others (Figure 6.5). As independent director, he spent time asking questions, probing, and resisting board colleagues in closing down discussions too early. Recognized for his intellect and his keen appreciation of issues, this director was particularly keen that more time should be spent together as a board better considering issues. He often highlighted that the mode of conversation did not encourage meaningful participation from board colleagues. He pointed out that although the CEO/chairman talked of listening and hearing, the reality was little listening and a great deal more talking at others. The quality of probing and reconsideration occurred when this director insisted that a point of conversation had not been fully examined. His responsiveness to other colleagues, sensitivity to their concerns as well as his appreciation of the long term, had this director dubbed as the "strategic healer." This director drew comparisons with other boards and other organizations predicting that with the board's way of working and quality of thinking, poor decisions

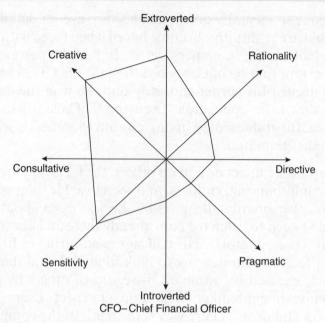

Figure 6.5   Strategic healer

would result and at some point in the future would disadvantage the organization.

The results of profiling were fed back to each individual and to the group at a special offsite board development day. The analysis of each of the profiles (no names on the maps) was followed by a team summary:

- Little commitment exists to the proposed acquisition;
- Whether the target acquisition is over priced or not, the board's ability to steward a post merger integration and management's capability to ensure for such integration, is suspect;
- Board dynamics substantially inhibit contribution from board members;
- Board dynamics are so dysfunctional that the majority of board members remain silent and tacitly agree to propositions they consider suspect;
- Full examination of issues does not take place;
- Management consider the board to be dysfunctional and of limited value;

- Little thought is given to the impact of one board member on the other allowing a practice to emerge of pushing through proposals and viewpoints irrespective of the contribution of the other;
- Gaining the agreement of the CEO/chairman is all that is necessary;
- In order to proceed, the board should commit to full discussion of how they can improve as a team.

The group listened in silence and remained silent after the facilitator finished speaking. One of the board members broke the stillness in the room and, in front of the others, asked for further feedback on his map. Some of the others followed. The strategic healer was the first to comment on the team feedback, "So basically what you mean is that unless we improve on how we work as a board, we will allow mistakes to occur and as a board and organization we are really vulnerable?"

The facilitator nodded in agreement.

"But are you sure, is it not strength of argument or, in this case, the lack of it?" asked the CFO. "The one reason why there is not enough challenge and discussion is that people are not sure of their own case."

The CEO/chairman agreed and drew on examples from the past where contrary opinion had been offered but under scrutiny the case of other directors was concluded as weak.

"Weak, or not further challenged?" questioned the facilitator.

"Not further challenged," offered the strategic healer.

Despite the comment to the contrary, the CFO and CEO/chairman argued strongly that poor substance, not style, was the prime reason for lack of board member contribution. The facilitator suggested exploring the point and offered the group a short and easy-to-complete profiler examining leadership style. The exercise did not take long but the results were as surprising as the visioning map exercise.

The CFO emerged as competitive, aggressive, seemingly unwilling to compromise or accommodate others – no surprise. The

CEO/chairman's results shifted the group. Competitive, aggressive, and direct, the CEO/chairman also boasted high scores on being collaborative, listening, and inviting comment. The three switched-off and angry directors equally displayed high scores on being competitive and single minded, but also high scores on being overaccommodating and too conscious of the feelings of others and of themselves. The CFO described them as schizophrenic, switching from strong and assertive to people pleasers and vulnerable. Not quite; the scores strongly indicated that if the three could dominate a conversation, they would. Should a stronger personality enter the discussion, they would respond in a submissive manner, emotionally almost wanting to please the stronger party.

"You mean it's not our chairman, but our inability to maintain the conversation," queried one of the three. As she spoke, the disbelief over the results was evident in her face.

The discussion then veered to the validity of the instrument and of profiling in general. The facilitator intervened. "Yes, of course, no instrument is 100 percent valid and reliable. Also, a great deal depends on the interpretation of the results. However, what is important is how you feel. Be honest with yourselves, do these scores feel right? Have they captured you? Are they accurate?"

"I didn't like the message but are the scores accurate for me – they are! With certain people, am I too accommodating – I am!" It was the second of the three that spoke.

The conversation that followed veered from how discussions in the past were unsatisfactory and were prematurely concluded to an admission of poor quality decisions being made. The more the group entered into detail of previous meetings, the more openly views were expressed. Two of the three held themselves responsible for not adequately challenging and examining issues. Even the CFO admitted that his singular approach did little to build a high performing board. Shortly after the away day, the female director resigned. A successor was found. Six months later, the facilitator was invited to attend a board meeting and offer feedback on their progress. At the end of the meeting, he turned to the CEO/chairman and said, "What is so much better is that you invite those that did not participate to contribute. Of the few occasions when that does not happen, one of the team ensures that all speak."

The CEO/chairman suggested a further follow up, six months hence.

The acquisition was not successful. A rival bidder simply paid a few billion dollars more. The CEO/chairman was bruised by having lost out! The strategic healer supported his CEO/chairman stating that the rival's over payment has depleted his acquisition war chest and credit. "One downturn in the market and that guy is bankrupt." The board agreed. In fact, the board breathed a sigh of relief when the rival bid succeeded.

The lost acquisition was more than compensated for by the distinct improvement of board performance. Real listening was now taking place. The facilitator even introduced the team to the rich history underlying communication and use of words (see Discipline 4). The group even discussed Habermas's speech forms and explored the degree to which they asserted, probed, consulted each other, all in the name of improving the quality of decisions.

Profiling takes board development to a much greater depth than board assessment review check lists. That does not mean to say that structured board assessment review should not be pursued. The review exercise surfaces board members' experience of working together and the quality of their deliberations and decisions as well as highlighting areas for improvement. However, in order to dig out the deeper impact of the dynamics of the board on each director, their level of contribution, and decision making and taking, a more penetrating approach is required. Profiling takes board review and assessment to the point of showing how each individual thinks and acts, making that evident to all other member of the group. It is at this point that the question, "do you as an individual and as a team, wish to change?" can be really addressed. Board assessment and review focuses conversation at only the group level. Profiling draws out group and individual behavior and implicitly displays the level of responsibility each individual feels to make changes. Profiling emphasizes, "what are you going to do to improve yourself and us all?"

In whatever guise or form, it makes sense to review how effectively the board has functioned over the last year. Whatever the benefits for the board, the board also sets an example for the rest of the organization. Periodic and structured attention to improvement encourages a culture of performance enhancement throughout the enterprise.

However, a note of caution with profiling: not all boards require such intensity of analysis. Of those that do, not all are prepared for deep individual and team scrutiny. In deciding whether to pursue profiling or not, the word capability is of particular relevance.

- Are the board members capable of entering into penetrating examination of the dynamics of their board?
- Are the board members emotionally able to face up to the reality of how they see the world, how the "world" sees them, and subsequently behave?
- Do board members require development in resilience, robustness, and confidence in order to more meaningfully discuss the outcomes of profiling?

Both board assessment review and profiling do not surface new data. Most on the board will have a view on what the board and each individual needs to do to improve. The challenge is of talking about what is already known: the deeper the level of discussion, the greater the challenge. Profiling is simply a more intense board review process and requires a greater level of courage to participate in order for the individual and the team to benefit. Thus, pursuing interviews with each board member prior to a profiling exercise and ascertaining the capability levels of the board is advised. Not only is each of the board member better prepared for the encounter but his or her capability to discuss what was previously not discussable has been improved. Certain groups cognizant of the need for profiling quickly enter into the exercise. Others may need six months of confidence and resilience boosting to enable them to benefit.

Director development

The purpose of board assessment review is to improve board performance improvement, from which naturally, each director benefits. However, individual director development is something above and beyond board development. Each person on a board may have quite separate development requirements.

"It is experience based but training may help," observes Derek Bonham, referring to board membership. Under wise chairmanship, contribution to the board and development as a director go hand in hand. However, Derek Bonham also points out that certain fundamentals of board directorship require additional attention. "When you're offered a position on a board, you sort of grab it," says Bonham. "You don't necessarily understand the legal consequences of what it is you're doing. So, I think there needs to be some sort of induction programme that reminds you of your legal obligations and board structures and ways of working."

Derek Bonham champions a commonly held view of "get the framework right, and from thereon much depends on experience.

Others argue on behalf of more personalized offsite director development. "Some of these people need to understand their duties as a director," says Jeremy Pope. "However they also need to separate their interests as a member producer from their duties to the board, to the organization, to the employees, to the membership and their corporate responsibilities," referring particularly to the boards of cooperatives.

Jeremy Pope draws attention to a critical question of director development: is reliance on experience sufficient?

Research at both board and management levels emphasizes the influence of context. Yes, experience is great. Even learning from mistakes is valuable, if not a dangerous path to tread. But any one person can become too familiar with their surroundings, limiting their mental boundaries of probing to the point where the person is not fully aware of their own limitations.

Two Cranfield researchers, Martin Clarke and David Butcher, challenge the view of relying solely on experience. Their research on democracy in organizations and the encouragement of innovation strongly affirms the need for organizing for new experiences. Go somewhere else, away from the people and context that is familiar and rethink. Mixing with different directors of different backgrounds, from different sectors and organizations of a considerably different structure and complexity, forces the individual to reexamine his or her assumptions. Murray Steele, another Cranfield colleague, who runs the board director development program, agrees. Intensive contemplation cannot be accomplished in one day. More time is needed.[3]

Development of the chairman

The area given least attention for development is that of chairmanship. What qualifies you to become a chairman?

"Breadth of Corporate experience is a prerequisite but crucially having served your apprenticeship as a non executive director and chairing important Committees as a non executive director – as well as developing a natural disposition for the role," says Sir John Parker.

Probing John Parker on the characteristics of "natural disposition," drew out qualities such as listening, humility, not desiring the limelight, resilience, and portraying "quiet calm." Working through, in a disciplined manner, the challenges facing the board, and the organization, in order to focus and understand the problems at hand and not be sidetracked, is just as important. Parker's response to the question, can such qualities be developed? "Of course, but where to go other than rely on yourself and learn from other great chairmen?"

And that is the problem, where to go?

Our research highlights three avenues for chairman development; feedback from the board, regular attendance to chairman networks, and opportunistic learning. Considered the most impactful is feedback from the board.

"You cannot sit in the middle of a circle and the board give you feedback. For the experience to be valuable, considerable thought is necessary concerning what opinions are captured, by whom and how that information is discussed with the chairman," says James Parkel

Parkel draws on the services of the LID to conduct the chairman's review. "The lead independent director is respected by the board and the chair. Whatever difficult messages need to be given, people trust it will be done with tact and will be constructive."

The SID role seems less well harnessed for such purposes – in the United Kingdom at least. Sir John Parker says:

> A tremendous opportunity exists in using the services of the senior independent director to gather the views of the board members and quietly sit with you and discuss the findings. I know this person will help me and is enthused with the opportunity to do so. So many more boards would benefit but seem reluctant to do so.

Our research confirms Parker's realization that the services of the SID could be much better utilized for both board and chairman benefit.

Pat Molloy considers the Nominations Committee as a suitable vehicle for board and director development. According to Molloy:

> The Nominations Committee are the people who should conduct the exercise. I consult the Nominations Committee; get their views on the board. I would then try and talk to every individual director, at least once a year, about their performance. I give them frank feedback if I feel that's in their best interests and in the best interests of the company.

Molloy, conscious of the trend to employ external facilitators, prefers to keep board assessment, review, and development in house. The reason? Who knows the board and its directors better than the chairman and who is better positioned to recommend contract renewal? "You will not get another three year term unless the Nominations Committee is happy with your performance of the first three years ... So there are the break points, a fairly rigorous assessment of performance to satisfy continuation," he says.

Others call upon external facilitation. Whatever the avenue, chairmen derive substantial benefit from structured and systematic performance review. It matters little whether the process is facilitated by an experienced and trusted director or by an external third party. What matters is that the chairman and the board trust the process and the person conducting the review.

We recommend subdividing feedback on the performance of the chairman into four categories, personal style, personal qualities, concern for risk, and, more broadly, chairman performance.

With each exercise, the spread of scores from members' responses should be highlighted and the mean score per scale identified. On this basis, the chairman is given the opportunity to consider his or her overall impact, explore in which areas he or she scores least, and where greatest variance of scores have emerged. Should one of the senior directors accept the responsibility for

Chairman audit checklist

Style	Mean Score		
The chairman	Not at all true		Very true
1. Encourages open debate	1 2	[3] 4	5
2. Summarizes well	1 2 3	[4	5]
3. Captures the essence of argument	1 [2	3] 4	5
4. Is easy to talk to	1 2 3	[4	5]
5. Raises sensitive issues	1 2	[3	4] 5
6. Handles tensions/sensitivities well	1 2 3	[4	5]
7. Works well with the CEO[a]	1 [2	3	4] 5
8. Is disciplined	1 2	[3	4] 5
9. Encourages consensus	1 2	[3] 4	5
10. Promotes teamwork	1 2	[3	4] 5
11. Uses teamwork to stifle debate	1 [2	3] 4	5
12. Operationally, becomes too involved	1 [2	3	4] 5

Mean score =

Qualities	Mean score				
The chairman	Not at all true			Very true	
1. Takes a long-term view	1	2	3	[4	5]
2. Is trustworthy	1	2	[3	4	5]
3. Displays integrity	1	[2	3	4]	5
4. Encourages challenge	[1	2	3	4	5]
5. Is persistent	1	2	[3	4]	5
6. Acts as a role model for others	1	2	3	[4	5]
7. Is robust	1	2	3	[4	5]

Mean score =

Risk	Mean score				
The chairman	Not at all true			Very true	
1. Promotes risk management thinking	[1	2]	3	4	5
2. Drives through risk management protocols	1	2	3	[4	5]
3. Enhances awareness of corporate reputation	1	[2	3]	4	5
4. Identifies corporate reputation vulnerabilities	1	2	3	[4	5]
5. Emphasizes shareholder relations	1	2	[3	4]	5

Mean score =

Performance	Mean score				
The chairman	Not at all true			Very true	
1. Displays little concern for shareholders	1	[2	3	4]	5
2. Effectively evaluates the performance of the CEO[b]	1	2	[3	4]	5
3. Effectively evaluates the performance of board members	1	2	3	[4]	5
4. Evaluates the performance of the board as a whole	1	2	[3]	4	5
5. Encourages feedback on his/her performance	1	2	3	[4	5]
6. Clarifies the skills/experience required of each board member	1	2	3	[4	5]
7. Utilizes well the skills/experience of board members	1	2	[3	4]	5
8. Determines the spread of skills/experience required on the board	1	2	3	[4	5]

Continued

Continued

Performance The chairman	Mean score				
	Not at all true			Very true	
9. Is professional in the search for CEO replacement[c]	1	2	3	4	5
10. Is professional in the search for board member replacement	1	2	3	4	5
11. Calls upon the most senior of the directors to intervene when necessary	1	2	3	4	5
12. Respects the intervention of the most senior of the directors	1	2	3	4	5
13. Jointly determines board agenda with the most senior of the directors	1	2	3	4	5
14. Asks board members to determine items for the board agenda	1	2	3	4	5
15. Discusses sensitive issues with the most senior of the directors	1	2	3	4	5
16. Displays concern for shareholders	1	2	3	4	5

Mean score =

Note:

[a] In the United States substitute CEO for Lead Independent Director (for most companies).

[b] In the United States substitute CEO for Lead Independent Director (for most companies).

[c] In the United States this will not apply for most companies as that role is adopted by the Lead Independent Director.

3, 4 | Example of spread of scores.

chairman facilitation, helpful examples can be offered of behavior and encounters at previous board meetings, crystallizing the point made in the check list. A third party facilitator may not have such a knowledge base to draw upon but has the independence to probe and challenge more deeply than a board colleague, who needs to sustain the relationship with the chairman.

Depending on the chairman's desire and/or need for development, an additional checklist is offered capturing how the board has benefited from the chairman's leadership.

Similarly, the span of scores from board members should be identified, as well as the average mean score. The purpose of the Chairman's leadership of the board checklist is to stimulate reflection not only on the chairman's style but also on the direct impact the individual has on the board. In this way, a more direct link can be drawn between aspects of personal style, personal qualities, and behavior with outcomes. The task of offering

Chairman's leadership of the board checklist

The chairman's leadership is such that the board	Mean score				
	Not at all true			Very true	
1. Benefits from the chairman's/CEO's or chairman's contribution[a]	1	2	3	4	5
2. Is diligent in governance application	1	2	3	4	5
3. Is attentive to corporate reputation	1	2	3	4	5
4. Is attentive to risk management	1	2	3	4	5
5. Performs effectively	1	2	3	4	5
6. Is well balanced in terms of member skill/experience	1	2	3	4	5
7. Is divided	1	2	3	4	5
8. Benefits from the Lead Independent Director contribution (SID in the United Kingdom)	1	2	3	4	5
9. Challenges the chairman/CEO or chairman when necessary	1	2	3	4	5
10. Has clear criteria for board member replacement	1	2	3	4	5
11. Emphasizes enhancing shareholder relations	1	2	3	4	5

Mean score =

Note:

[a] Chairman/CEO for US Boards; chairman for non-US boards.

additional feedback, not captured by the checklists, is now made that much easier.

Picking your guru

"I am accustomed to executive coaching. I think it's a very good thing. In fact, when at Vickers when we totally transformed the company, we benefited greatly from working with an executive coach," says Sir Colin Chandler.

The final leg to board development is calling upon a third party adviser, sometimes referred to as a coach. Similar to Sir Colin Chandler, Don Argus calls on the services of a variety of professionals ranging from professional search to board and director development. "We use external people. We search the world for the skill we want," he says.

The use of external advisers extends beyond search, training, and development to support of key functions as information and communication technology as well as investment and merger and acquisitions advice. Paul Myners, in a *Financial Times* article offers three guidelines for choosing the right adviser:[4]

- Choose the person not the employing institution;
- Concentrate on the intellectual firepower of the adviser(s), not the size, grandeur, or boutique nature of the institution for which he or she works;
- Don't haggle; pay for the quality of advice needed.

A fourth point requires inclusion. By all means choose the adviser. But in so doing, choose the adviser that understands you and the organization. Sensitivity to context, sensitivity to critical relationships, appreciation of what the organization needs to do bearing in mind its competitive position in the market place and economic life cycle and understanding how far you, as the client, can be taken, are important concerns for hiring valuable advisory support.

In the development of the board and of the organization, that critical and helpful input from an external source can make an invaluable contribution to performance improvement. Knowing what and who can fit in and still challenge the organization, displays a high understanding of context. Misread context and no developmental initiative will succeed. Accurately capture context and the willingness to improve is evident.

In addition, a minority of chairmen make personal arrangements.

"I am a member of a chairmen's club. It's run by a consulting company," one chairman told us.

Yet, few chairmen are members of particular networks that offer development. Learning for the greater majority is opportunistic, attending dinners or meetings where a speaker or topic of interest is on the agenda.

Most freely admit that they gain through constructive board-related feedback exercises and after that little further development is pursued. "We ought to be running a series of masterclasses, getting people who are considered the outstanding chairman to run the masterclass with those who have the ambition and insight to be chairmen. Give people insights on what it means to be chairman, what kinds of issues to face, what kind of problems to face, how to deal with people," suggests John Phillips.

The transition factor

The development issue is particularly important at the earliest stages in a chairman's appointment. New chairmen or directors have to learn about their new surroundings and the intimate but unspoken nuances that powerfully influence whether the new person will be accepted. Existing board members learn about the new appointee, how they think and feel, their strengths, their vulnerabilities and, most of all, whether they can contribute. Aside from personal acceptance, what real contribution is required from the newcomer? As a board member, how long will it take them to identify where is the position of the firm in its economic lifecycle and from that insight, what is the competitive advantage of the enterprise, how is it differentiated, and then to conclude what valuable contribution can the board and its directors make?

The more dramatic the change of role, change of location, and change of industry, the steeper and lengthier the learning. In effect, the newly appointed chairman or board member has to release themselves from old habits and assumptions, become immersed in the new context, recognize and respond to those hidden messages, and relearn new capabilities and ways of working.

An *Economist* article reports an all time high of US CEO departures, 1322 in 2005.[5] Getting into the job now has to take place in less than the much cited first 100 days. That is a daunting challenge and has led to the emergence of a new phenomenon – on-boarding. This involves picking the right person, getting that person deeply into the firm, and better ensuring their success. The secret to on-boarding is preboarding. Forget about developing high quality executive relationships,

"A new boss should ideally have picked his new team and have a communication strategy – if not a fully worked out business plan – in place on his first day into the job," reports *The Economist* on preboarding.

Preboarding is the period between accepting the job and the first day of starting. It involves the following:

- identifying those relationships that the new boss considers critical;
- identifying the shadow board, those individuals that really pull the strings;
- identifying those top managers who could damage future relationships or feel negative because they have been passed over;
- knowing who is wanted even before starting the job and know what is wanted from them.[6]

While the transitional experience extends considerably over 100 days and prepreparation helps, it does so only up to a point.

The concept of transition goes back to the original 1960s research conducted by Elizabeth Kubler-Ross, in the sphere of medicine, not business.[7] The research aimed to help patients come to terms with terminal illness. The ups and downs of such traumatic learning were later discovered to parallel the experiences of managers having to face the relearning of how to become accomplished in their new appointment (Figure 6.6). The greater the change, the deeper and more profound the learning curve experience and the greater the length of time to readjust. Having knowledge of the new job and being a member of the organization is of considerable help in negotiating through the transitional experience.

For those that change organization, change industry, and especially those that are new to senior roles and the corporate center, their transitional timeframe could extend to even 25 months. Whatever mistakes, namely operational errors of judgment are made, they are likely to be made within the first 100 days. However, more serious strategic misjudgment may only be evident two or three years hence. Misreading people or the dynamics of the board can lead to unnecessarily damaging senior relationships. Misinterpreting the politics of the board or the organization and not fully appreciating the values and cultural habits of the organization may lead to change that has little chance of succeeding. Such sensitive errors undermine winning hearts and minds, the gaining of credibility, and being trusted. The greater the dissonance created by the new person, the more likely others are unwilling to hear. A newly appointed chairman may have quickly grasped what should be the role of the board in supporting a change of business imperative to drive through the organization. However, owing to his or her not having grasped cultural nuances, the new chairman is not trusted and disliked. The temptation of others is to undermine the individual's vision as well as their position.

Maturing into the role is an absolute must. Research confirms that exceptionally talented learners, exhibiting the qualities of listening, humility, admitting to their mistakes, and controlling their ego, can negotiate through their transition within a three-month period. Yet, this is less than 10 percent of the executive and independent director population. The greater majority

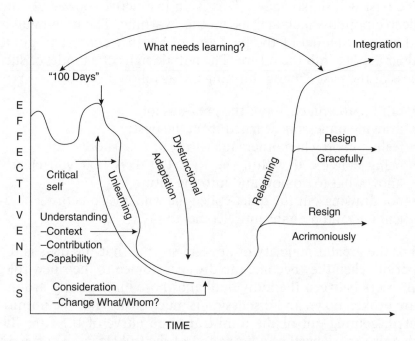

Figure 6.6 Transition curve: board members 12–18 months

require 12–25 months. The average transition time for newly appointed chairmen varies between 12–18 months, as it does also for board members. The more the new chairman is also new to the board, the more likely the learning curve timeframe will extend to 18 months. The more the new chairman has been a member of the board, the more likely the transition time will be 12 months or less. Familiarity with context is key. There are three phases to transitional learning (see Figure 6.6).

Phase 1: the first 100 days

Sometimes known as the honeymoon period, the first 100 days involve simply becoming accustomed to the new role. Confidence is high. The exhilaration of starting the new job breeds excitement in others. The compliments flow thick and fast. And that is the first warning; others expect more than can be realized.

Enjoying the attention, the new chairman may make an assumption to be later deeply regretted, that what achieved success in the past will do so again. This is an instinctive, powerful, and deep emotion which acts as another warning. The individual is allowing a model of the past and of another context to guide their actions into the future. The telltale signs of a model of success of the past driving thinking are as follows:

- talking too much about the previous job;
- drawing on lessons learned from the past;
- feeling good when others refer to your past successes;
- being convinced within the first 100 days that you clearly know what to do now and into the future;
- not drawing out the quiet colleague who has something challenging, and perhaps unwelcome, to say.

For the greater majority of appointees, the first 100 days is the period when they become rapidly accustomed to their new role. Barriers between the individual and those immediately around are broken down and discussion is much easier. For the uninitiated, coming out of the mini-transition curve of the first 100 days is experienced as coming out of the full learning curve. In fact, the transitional experience has just begun.

Phase 2: unlearning

In this phase the underlying reality of the challenges to be faced slowly surface. For the other board members, the idiosyncrasies of the newly appointed chairman now become evident. Critical is whether there is a meeting of minds on the prime challenges facing the chair, the board, and the enterprise. To have a fundamental difference of view between the chairman and the board on the contribution desired from the chair leads to deep and even bitter tension. Personal warmth and affinity does little to compensate for differences on prime purpose. It is at this point that many new appointees realize that the skills and capabilities that worked in the past may no longer be appropriate. Change is needed in the person's skill portfolio.

Coming to terms with the breadth of adjustment required is not easy. For the new appointee, what needs to be done to the board and organization may be glaringly obvious. Colleagues well entrenched on the board and in the organization may not be of the same view. The feeling of having to accommodate the wishes of others is irritating. The new chairman may feel sidelined from achieving his or her goals. To do nothing is of little help. To do something and be isolated is also of little help. Winning over colleagues and the building of a new confidence in the team, even reshaping the team, is important.

How to do that? The understanding of context and the nature of contribution required from the new chairman, as well as existing board members, has to be matched by attention to capability development and adjustment of personal style so as to better fit in. Fitting in is an elusive concept. Each person has their own idea of what that really means. Fitting in could undermine introducing necessary change. Considerations of what and whom to change have to run in parallel with a critical look at yourself – what is it that I need to change in myself to make a success of this job?

Questions that require consideration are as follows:

- To what extent are the accountabilities, authorities, and responsibilities for the new incumbent's role, or for that matter any role, on the board well aligned bearing in mind what needs to be achieved?

- To what extent are others, well established in their role, accepting or deflecting accountability for their own responsibilities and for how long has such practice continued?
- What do performance effectiveness, fitting in, or value-adding contribution really mean to the board, or broader, to the organization?
- To what extent do others expect a particular style to be exhibited by the new chairman that is in keeping with past practice?
- To what extent is the new individual able or comfortable to switch styles in order to make an impact on the board?
- What do board members and senior management really need to learn in order that change can be successfully introduced?

The individual may have walked into a culture of honesty. Responsibilities, authorities, and accountabilities are well aligned. Each top director holds himself or herself accountable for what he or she do. Accountability is not just a structural tool but it is fundamentally a state of mind – "I am responsible for what I do or say." A more dysfunctional way of operating is to deflect accountability, blame someone else. Contextual reality may be that of a negative culture. Emotions of threat, anxiety, insecurity, nondisclosure, and denial may be rife. Directors say one thing but mean something else.

For the newly appointed chairman, additional questions require reflection:

- Do the board members share comparable views on the prime purpose of the board and the value it adds to the organization?
- To what extent are relationships on the board positive and enabling or undermining and dysfunctional?
- To what extent does attention to "personalities" on the board divert attention from addressing business, risk and governance issues?

Each board, each management team has its own unique character. Learning how to interact with new board colleagues, how to interface with executive management without undermining the CEO, and how to monitor, support, and, if necessary, discipline the CEO, in each new situation, is challenging but crucial to do.

At this critical second stage of transition, unlearning involves standing back from previous assumptions and instincts concerning best and desired practice and recognizing the true nature of the new context.

The breakthrough in learning is the full realization of the meaning held by the others on the board of the term "effectiveness." Effectiveness is an equally elusive, but deeply sensitive, concept. Learning what is difficult to raise, who can be offended and over what, and what are the undisclosed expectations concerning the new chairman's or board director's contribution requires sensitivity and tact.

Recognizing how contextual sensitivities impact on board and business performance draws the new chairman to a further set of questions:

- What should I be thinking differently?
- What should I be doing differently?
- What should they be thinking and doing differently?
- Who around here is going to change – me or them?

However the new board is perceived, any new appointee is going to have to go through some personal change – change of style, change of thinking, change of business model, even rethinking how to introduce change but change if for no other reason than to earn the respect of the new board and management. Yet, some resent having to change.

We have heard chairmen complain: "Why should I change? I am not the one with the problem. They need to change." This sentiment may be accurate, but is contextually unworkable. During the period of unlearning and detaching oneself from the successes and experiences of the past, consideration of how to adapt must run in parallel. Resisting how to adjust, the individual goes round in circles – what's the problem; who has to change; what has to change; why do I have to change? – it is not me they have to change. And so the cycle starts once more. Once personal adjustment is allowed for, the individual enters phase three of the transition curve.

Phase 3: relearning

Lessons from the past are now intermingled with new ways of working. The individual is more realistic about what he or she needs to do. Having come to terms with the underlying attitudes, values, and behavior, on the board and in the organization, the person, particularly as director, less so as chairman, may realistically recognize that to prolong his or her stay achieves little. The best way forward is to resign; the question is whether that should be gracefully or acrimoniously achieved. So much depends on the quality of due diligence prior to accepting the role and the frustrations experienced through the period of unlearning. The degree to which relationships have been tarnished and the depth of mistakes made dictate whether premature departure is a smooth or disturbing experience.

Alternatively, Phase 2 could be well handled. Assuming a consolidation of learning, the individual forcefully stamps his or her personality on his or her role. Others respect the individual's efforts to learn. Having won credibility, greater listening to new ideas is taking place. Rethinking the challenges facing the board and the organization, how to enable management through better quality strategic proposals, and redesigning governance application become central topics of conversation for the board. The new chairman, or board member, is here to stay. A new philosophy runs through the board.

Growing the talent pool

Executive succession was commonly discussed by our research participants. One chairman we spoke to said he considers it his duty as chairman to vet and, if necessary, initiate programs of management development and succession for key posts. He is right to do so. The fact is that future board talent will be scarcer.

"It's becoming more difficult. More and more people are saying it's not worth it. It's not just about money. It's the responsibility; the learning curve to be climbed. There are a lot more interesting things to do with their lives. A critical reason is legal culpability," observes Pat Molloy.

Bernard Rethore concurs: "The pool is slowly drying up. Talent is going to private equity. Less constraining, more fun and certainly not the same governance constraints."

Pat Molloy, conscious of ever greater governance demands and the danger of a box ticking mentality, emphasizes making board work interesting: "The challenge is to make sure that it's not boring and that it's an enjoyable experience. We've managed a lot of change and brought a lot of new people on board. It's fun."

Others disagree with the basic premise of the board talent pool diminishing. "Once you look beyond the typical CEO pool, you'll find that there is no shortage of highly qualified people to sit on boards. As long as there is a meaningful role to play, they will serve and contribute. The key is to get the right mix of people and skills to complement the organization's needs," says Kelly O'Dea. Herbert Müller agrees and sees no shortage of good applicants for positions on the German two-tier supervisory board. "It is for many people a matter of honour and prestige to be invited to sit on a board of an important company. You build your network. You get inside another business. To rotate out of operating responsibilities and gain experience, is invaluable. Also the money is better."

Aside from status, Herbert Müller identifies the benefits of growing one's network and extending one's portfolio of skills of experience. Rather than being a limiting experience, Herbert Müller sees boards as fertile grounds for training and development.

Whether the talent pool is diminishing or not, most in our research agree that identifying future talent and creating the opportunities for development is a prime responsibility of the chairman. Many chairmen offer the view that becoming intimately acquainted with the high flyers in the ranks of management is critical to identifying and developing board talent.

"The board can get a feeling … they would be involved in some of the IMI (Irish Management Institute) presentations, where our young people have presented the business case for their project. The board members have a feeling for the talent that is there and have the opportunity to meet younger management," says Ronnie Kells.

Familiarity and acquaintance with rising talent provides opportunity for experienced board members, through their network, to refer particular individuals to the boards of others. Sir John Parker goes one step further:

> When I and the board see some of our high flyers, we take it upon ourselves to place some of our future top managers as non execs on someone else's board. All that have experienced sitting on a board state that they have benefited immeasurably. We gain from their development and, overall, a new generation of board directors are now being fed into the market.

Even so, much depends on the mind-set of the chairman. Those positive about developing future board talent recognize that attendance of a formal course or becoming a member of some other board pays dividend but does not necessarily offer a direct payback.

Key points

- World-class boards invest substantially in the development of their directors and senior managers.
- One of the most commonly adopted development techniques is that of board assessment and review – including questionnaire surveys, structured interviews, and focus groups.
- It is popular to combine board performance assessment questionnaires with interviews.

$\rightarrow$

- Profiling is an emerging tool for board and director performance assessment. Profiling involves in-depth explanation of the mind-set of each board member, and how his or her way of being affects his or her and the board's performance and contribution. Feedback from profiling needs to be offered at both the individual and group level.
- Before adopting profiling as a tool for board and director development, assessment of the capability of the board to benefit from the technique is important. If the board members cannot cope with profiling, the chairman should either prepare them or not adopt this approach.
- It is the chairman's responsibility to consider the channels for development for each of the directors on the board.
- It is also the chairman's responsibility to consider appropriate avenues for his or her own development, which can include using the SID or LID, calling upon external facilitation and advice, or joining certain clubs or meetings.
- It is up to each board director to realistically recognize the time required for transition and the depth of learning necessary, when joining a new board.
- It is the chairman's responsibility to guide new board members through the depths of their learning curve.
- Understanding of the three phases of learning assists a director to successfully negotiate his or her transition.
- It is the chairman's responsibility to grow the talent pool of future board directors, particularly as opinion exists that the talent pool is diminishing.

On being world class: The six disciplines at work

> World-class chairmen give leadership and select a world class board that's balanced and makes a valid contribution.
>
> Lord Tom Sawyer

What does it mean to be a world-class chairman? The simple answer is that it means you are able to create and maintain a world-class board. That begs the question what is a world-class board – and that is hard to define.

"A world class board is recognized as such by those involved – management, board directors, press, shareholders, analysts," says Gareth Davis. "A first rate board is where people are comfortable with each other. You can have robust challenge without anybody taking offence. There's such a feeling of trust and integrity," adds Derek Bonham.

What is clear from our research is that trust, transparency, and discipline are the three essential elements of good corporate governance. They are the hallmarks of a world-class board – and a world-class chairman. As the previous chapters have shown, the best chairmen achieve these goals through mastery of the six disciplines:

1. Discipline 1: delineating boundaries
2. Discipline 2: sense making
3. Discipline 3: interrogating the argument
4. Discipline 4: influencing outcomes
5. Discipline 5: living the values
6. Discipline 6: developing the board.

In the end, though, the disciplines are a means to an end not an end in themselves. The end is the creation of a world-class board.

It sounds somewhat tautological, but being world class means being recognized as world class. Whatever the characteristics of a world-class board are, they also need to be felt. If a sufficient number of significant stakeholders feel (and sometimes not even adequately describe) the board to be outstanding in value contribution and performance, then it probably is.

Gareth Davis's notion of a shared feeling of outstanding performance is significant. Numerous top managers, board members, and significant observers acclaim particular boards, but cannot put their finger on why an outstanding contribution has occurred. Observation, however, of boards recognized as world class suggest they are clear on five key issues. These are the criteria by which the chairman must be judged.

First, they understand their prime purpose and contribution.

Second, they strive to attain a balanced board, through effective succession planning and capability building.

Third, they take governance very seriously, including codes of conduct (even where they choose not to follow guidelines), the role of senior and lead independent directors, and board tenure.

Fourth, they constantly review their integrity on executive remuneration and other issues.

And fifth, they translate these concerns into action by defining and living up to their ethical standards: in other words, they hold themselves and others accountable.

This final chapter explores the characteristics of world-class boards – and by inference world-class chairmen.

Clarity of purpose

The reality is that, beyond the obvious governance role, the contribution of the board will vary according to the circumstances facing the company. Clarity of purpose relies on a good understanding of what is happening on the ground and in the company's markets. That is rarely gained by sitting in an oak-paneled boardroom.

"It is helpful to go to various businesses to see how they see what they are doing. It gives you the opportunity to question what they think about the world and how they see the role of head office, whether it is interfering, or helping them," notes Derek Bonham.

Derek Bonham's explanation of how lower management view the contribution of the corporate center (head office and the board) is particularly apposite. Our study suggests that many of those serving on boards do not know how they can best contribute. For example:

- 85 percent of UK board directors cannot clearly identify or agree between themselves how the organization, on whose board they sit, is differentiated from the competition or what is the firm's competitive advantage. The last seven years of study unearths the considerable variance of opinion that exists between colleagues on the same board concerning competitive advantage, differentiation, and what adds value.
- 90 percent of US board members reported to us that they feel themselves distant from the management of the firm, as much arising from Sarbanes–Oxley requirements that they maintain an impartial view. The net result is similar to British boards: poor shared view (as a board) on competitive advantage and differentiation.

Lack of clarity concerning the prime purpose of the firm emerges from our study as a big issue. The best boards know how they add value, but many mediocre boards do not. Every chairman should think about the following:

- How many boards devote time to examining their own value-adding contribution – to focus on their purpose and contributions?
- How many boards even discuss different opinions on how the board adds value?

- If board members were directed to state their value and contribution, would the responses be idiosyncratic or related to competitive advantage?

Our survey results lean towards idiosyncrasy, often determined by some past experience of success in some other organization. Penetrating the heart of the corporation in order to determine the specific requirement for monitoring and supervision is one aspect of distinguishing the extraordinary from the ordinary board.

Bringing balance to the board

Diversity and balance are two sides of the same coin. Boards need diversity of perspective – including alternative functional, cultural, and psychological points of view. But they must also be balanced. In the past, western boards were dominated by white Anglo-Saxons. That is now changing.

Diversity is a word that we heard many times during our research. "Diversity in all senses: from asking appropriate questions to capturing the expertise needed. We need a Russian board member. Our market in Russia is growing and we must have the right people," said a UK chairman in the business of minerals extraction.

"The board has to have balance," says Gareth Davis. "If you are doing business in Asia, you should have someone with Asian experience on your board. Now, what Asian? It is the Asian that has the background and capabilities to help you. It's all geared to the agenda of the business and the board's role in taking the business forward."

A world-class chairman understands that a clear and shared understanding of the business drives board configuration and the necessary skills and competencies of its members.

However, the distinction drawn between competencies and capabilities is often not fully appreciated. World-class boards go out of their way to make the distinction clear. The nominations committee, and/or the chairman, provides insightful examination of the value and necessity of each role. The outcome of those deliberations is presented to the board for approval. The reason for each role on the board and the background, track record, and skill profile of each member is periodically presented as evidence for scrutiny.

Identifying capable directors

"It's all about capabilities. Oh, you've just got a woman on your board. Oh, that's a tick in the box. That is an absolute insult, (a) to the board and, (b) to the woman. Directors should be selected purely on capability," says Gareth Davis.

Gareth Davis is absolutely right. As we have seen, capability assessment raises the question of "how capable are you of using your skills and competencies in a way that makes a difference here today?"

Capability determination is a matter of context. It is also a matter of timing – this person is right for us now, but we will need other perspectives going forward. Next year things may be different. This is who we want now and, hopefully, together we will grow.

The more senior the role, the more capability considerations predominate. The most skillful may not always be the best. The board has to function. Being conversant with the required professional and technical competencies is important. Attention to relationships and the winning of argument with the full support of colleagues predominate.

Thus, role and member profiling leads naturally to the question of succession – an issue that until recently has been neglected.

Serious about succession planning

Succession planning is another increasingly important area that world-class chairmen attend to. There are a number of dimensions to this. One is being honest about recruiting new directors.

Consider the following example. The directors of a large international, US registered company agreed that additional expertise in the area of energy was needed on the board. Together with the help of a search consultant, a specific role brief was drafted. The search for suitable candidates began. The chairman/CEO desired someone with appropriate experience but, as a person, who would also challenge. The one quality the board lacked was challenge. Why? This was because of the dominance of the chairman/CEO. Potentially suitable candidates were found but after informal discussions with the chairman and certain nomination committee members, declined to pursue the position further. The other board members knew all too well why. By the third candidate bowing out of the race, the chairman consulted the headhunter. The two had developed an open relationship.

"It is a matter of style. This board is powerful but challenge isn't one of its qualities," commented the search consultant.

This was not a new conversation. The consultant had a sufficiently robust understanding with the chairman to offer his honest views. "The way the board works is unlikely to change. You need someone of suitable experience and background but also who fits. It's a matter of style and personality. Perhaps an ex-public servant more accustomed with offering advice? It is important to just be honest. In order for things to work, just be honest about who fits here."

The chairman agreed. The search unearthed two former UK diplomats. The one appointed, although experienced, was not the most impressive in terms of track record and experience concerning energy. However, he fits in and works comfortably with chairmen.

The chairman in the case above may not have encouraged open discourse but, as a person, was extremely able. Neither the board nor the organization was ready for him to leave. Above all else, the newly appointed independent director had to fit. In fact, the attraction of diplomats for board positions is recognized. There has been an exodus of diplomats to the private sector.[1]

Succession planning also extends to the chairman himself. Interestingly, a *Financial Times* survey reported that, "fewer than one in three FTSE 350 boards have a plan for handling the succession of the chairman."[2] Board succession planning faces the uncomfortable challenge of who raises the subject with the in situ chairman? Whoever raises the issue faces being labeled as wanting to be the next chairman. Should the topic be raised, that NED's tenure may well be curtailed. The greatest challenge is to discuss succession with a chairman with a track record of success. Many of the chairmen interviewed recognized the problem but on someone else's board. Only a few initiated serious discussion of their successor.

That is changing. Succession will become a more central agenda. The *Financial Times* reports recent research by the headhunter Heidrick and Struggles, prominent in board director search, that lengthy transitions can be damaging.[3] Further, shareholders are becoming more vocal over succession. The eight months for Sir John Bond to succeed Lord MacLaurin as chairman of Vodafone is considered unacceptable. Shareholder activism requiring greater involvement of being kept better informed was clearly displayed at the Sainsbury pronouncement of Ian Prosser as chairman elect. Many in interview considered that protest pressured the supermarket retailer to reverse its decision.

For the chairman, or for that matter any role on the board, it falls upon the chairman to initiate the debate. "You have to balance knowing what more you can do with self belief. I prefer erring on being clear when my time is up. If you have led the board well, your colleagues are likely to tell you, 'please stay'!" says Sir John Parker.

Those with confidence are the first to raise the topic of succession. Preliminary discussion affirms whether or not more in-depth examination is required. If yes, the nominations committee can then take over. It is paramount to maintain the confidence of the shareholders. Paul Emerton, corporate governance manager at Schroders Bank, observes: "Where succession goes smoothly, it shows that the company has the confidence of the shareholders, that there is a good board and good processes in place."[4]

Beyond compliance: leading governance

Trust and transparency are two of the three aspects of governance, the third being discipline. All three are fundamental to managing issues such as executive remuneration (see later).

Sir John Parker recalls the views of the senior managers of National Grid who have accepted independent director posts on the boards of other companies. "You instil leading governance practices beyond complying," he says. According to Sir John Parker:

> Strong central financial control that penetrates all the way down to the lowest standing financial controller wherever he is sitting. There has to be a "dotted line" independent relationship right through to the boardroom. The documentation of our policies and procedures. The documentation of authorities that we are reliant upon. I know it sounds pretty bureaucratic but people know precisely what their authority is and they know how to get sign off.

Well understood financial controls, clear documentation of what to do and with what authority, should unambiguously stretch through the organization. Being systematic and disciplined about controls heightens the confidence of shareholders and other relevant stakeholders. Their investment in the company is well stewarded.

Sir John Parker's attention to disciplined governance stands out. Yet, our study shows a broad sweep of practice with US and Australian board directors more conscious than others of the need for continued, good governance. In Turkey and Russia, the term governance continues, at best, to be a mystery, and for most, an irritant. Divergence of governance practice occurs on UK boards, with some comparable to Sir John Parker of being "beyond compliant" and others at the knife-edge of facing litigation.

Governance and business performance are linked to that of rules and protocols guaranteeing the rights of stakeholders. A globally renowned champion of governance, Sir Adrian Cadbury, agrees. Addressing the 7th International Conference on

Corporate Governance, held in London (2006), Sir Adrian extended his 1991 definition of "the system by which companies are directed and controlled" to a framework which "should recognise the rights of stakeholders established by law or through mutual agreement and encourage active co-operation in creating wealth, jobs and the sustainability of financial sound enterprises."[5] The point being made is that the rules and protocols directly relevant to business performance, the governance of longevity, should extend to a broader concern for stakeholders, to the governance of sustainability.

At first glance the two terms, longevity and sustainability appear similar but in fact they are substantially different. Longevity refers to long lasting, something durable that endures and outlives. Sustainability, undoubtedly, holds a time connotation, but particularly refers to aid, assistance, championship, benevolence, and help. The protection, advocacy, and assistance of those at risk stand side by side with being there for a long time. From "keep the firm going" to "consciousness of the broader community and environment" covers the range of governance meanings prevalent today.

If sustainability is so much richer, why longevity? Well, longevity inadvertently emerged as a protection from 25 or more years of scandal. From the corporate raiders of the 1970s or 1980s, Alan Bond and Michael Milken to wrongdoing, BCCI, Maxwell's raiding of his own pension fund, Tyco, the governance concern with longevity protects the corporation through rules that guarantee transparency in order to trust the management. The governance of longevity specifically focuses on shareholders. They are not to be cheated and their investments are to be protected. If anything, the criticism of the governance of longevity is that it is swinging too far toward control for its own sake.

"While poor governance leads to low performance, good governance does not necessarily imply high corporate performance and returns," are the words of two academicians examining the effects of governance application.[6]

The following was reported in the *Financial Times* (Monday, July 10, 2006):[7] "British companies listed in New York are entering a crunch period this week as a Sarbanes-Oxley deadline passes and time constraints force some into compliance shortcuts."

Originally structured to counter corporate malfeasance and improve investor confidence, Sarbanes–Oxley, although having consolidated necessary control protocols, has been lambasted as cumbersome, expensive, and requiring unnecessary certifications. Specifically, Section 404 is causing the greatest anxiety. Still, some 1200 foreign companies need to comply: 40 percent Canadian; 25 percent European; 10 percent Asian; and 10 percent Latin American.[8] Even the US regulator, the Securities and Exchange Commission, is reported not to impose penalties on companies that are still not fully compliant but will require them to show what they are doing to address shortfalls. The *Financial Times* reports the objectives of Sarbanes–Oxley as laudable:

- improve the quality and accuracy of financial reporting;
- reduce fraud and fake accounting;
- raise awareness of internal controls;
- heighten executive responsibility;
- strengthen the independence of audit firms.

However, the downside is the red tape burden:

- asking auditors to attend internal control meetings to verify they have happened;
- document all office keys issued in recent years;
- ask employees to change their email password every month;
- minute all discussions on company accounts;
- ask auditors to scrutinize the dispatch of products to customers.

Many CEOs' and chairmen's comments about cost are understandable. "HSBC spent US$28.4m on Section 404 advisory work in its most recent financial year, while GlaxoSmithKline paid £2.4m. In France, Lafarge spent €10m last year and Veolia has spent €20–25m over the past three years."[9]

The other complaint is about the tedium and "unproductive" use of time on thinking through and introducing controls. Eric

Hutchinson, CFO of Spirent Communications captures a current and widely held sentiment:

> "We all get up, clean our teeth, and have a cup of tea. Well, imagine you have to document all that, explain any deviation from the normal routine and get your partner to certify it. ... And every now and again an auditor will come round to check you've done it. That's what it feels to be complying with Sarbanes-Oxley."[10]

Spirent Communications, a small company with a reported turnover of £340 million is also reported as spending £3 million a year on Sarbanes–Oxley. The critique of the *Financial Times* is of "over zealous box tickers who have not grasped the law's origins on intentions."[11]

Our study confirms current wisdom that beyond a certain point, greater attention to governance does not enhance business performance. Should performance, however, dip, the first area of scrutiny is why, and the second is governance, why did someone not react sooner?

A number of US outside (sometimes termed external) directors are of the opinion that Sarbanes has induced even greater inhibition at board level and as one suggested "even driving corruption more underground." Yet, there is little evidence that SOX (common but slangy abbreviation for Sarbanes–Oxley) will be repealed. It is here to stay as are other governance codes worldwide. The only sensible way forward is to learn to live with it. Some of our interviewees had even found cohabitation with SOX easier than they expected.

"I surprise myself but SOX has proved to be useful, more useful than I thought. I reluctantly admit that the benefits have outweighed the costs to this point," says Bernard Rethore.

Approached with a positive frame of mind, regulation can be used as an opportunity to introduce valuable disciplines into the enterprise. That view is now more readily supported,

"It's not Sarbanes that is suffocating businesses. It's Sarbanes done badly," observes Jonathan Wyatt, MD at Protiviti, a risk consultancy. "A lot of businesses didn't understand the requirements and didn't know where they were going, so they introduced a new form to be filled out and that becomes a major pain."[12]

World-class chairman leading world-class boards emphasize being more than compliant. Be ahead of the game. SOX is about the governance of longevity and there should be no debate about that point.

The bucks stop here: integrity checks

The best boards go well beyond simple compliance. They actively scan the horizon for the next best practice. They also ensure that integrity is not a hollow phrase but is constantly reviewed and championed. They recognize the vital role of key independent directors in this.

Harnessing the SIDs and LIDs

"The Lead Independent Director role is very helpful even though the lead independent can get rid of you. What's important is to sit down with the lead independent director and work out how to make the contribution," says John Berndt

Recognizing the fact that the lead independent director (LID) is not required to intervene unless CEO chairman performance falters, John Berndt views the LID as providing great assistance to the chairman.

Tony Alexander views the UK version, the senior independent director (SID), with greater skepticism. "It is quite an onerous obligation, because you are being brought in to umpire from time to time, but only when things are going wrong."

As we have noted, SIDs privately express reservations about their role and purpose. Both SIDs and chairmen acknowledge the potential contribution of the role. Both also report that little attention is given to the SIDs' better utilization.

"They are probably seen as a threat, but, if the truth be told, they are of invaluable help to the chairman. Codes won't help. The chairman has to define what is needed from the SID," says Sir John Parker.

Acknowledging the tension, Sir John Parker clarifies how to gain greater benefit from the SID:

- **Chairman takes the initiative**. The chairman identifies the level of support needed from the SID/LID.
- **Invite feedback**. Offer feedback to the chairman. John Berndt recommends after every board meeting, that the LID meet with the other independent, external board members and capture their concerns. These should be summarized and feedback provided to the chairman. Other chairmen follow suit asking the SID and LID to take an active role in board performance assessment, particularly that of inviting confidential comment on the performance and contribution of the chairman.
- **Offer counsel and support to the chairman**. However, the chairman positions the level of intimacy between the two.

Although in line with Sir John Parker, Tony Alexander also emphasizes greater proactivity from the SIDs/LIDs in scoping out their role.

"One thing you've got to be able to do is step out of the box and look back into the box from the point of view of the investors, and understand what it is they don't like and be able to convey that, convince your colleagues that something needs to be done."

The real hurdle is the discomfort of the SID. "You are drawn in by the major shareholder. Your natural instinct is to defend your colleagues who are probably your friends. But you have got to be able to stand aside. That's not easy."

The quality to remain independent is primary. Most SIDs/LIDs are aware of their responsibilities and of the strength of character needed to stand apart. "In an analysis of senior independent directors, you'd find a lot of them would be chairmen of other companies," says Tony Alexander. "They appreciate the pressures that are on the chairman."

Our study shows that the US LID more readily takes the initiative to shape his or her role and, if necessary, intervene. The UK SID emerges as grappling with the finer points of the role. Certainly, the chairman of the board not making better use of the SID is one factor. The other is exposure to the outside world. As the point of last resort for shareholders, SIDs are exposed to divided loyalties. As Tony Alexander notes, the challenge is more personal. Until that tension is openly aired, UK boards are likely to continue making poor use of their SIDs. It is the chairman who initiates the conversation of how to go about unearthing personal weaknesses.

Managing board tenure

Through code and legislation, board tenure is identified as an important aspect of governance. In the United Kingdom, the Higgs recommendation of two terms of office, each of three years, for the external board director is mirrored around the world. Why three years? It is in order to maintain independence. If they stay too long, independent directors can get too cozy with senior management. Certain studies confirm that view. Nikos Vafeas of the University of Cyprus reports that directors with lengthy tenure are more likely to support increased CEO remuneration than would otherwise be the case.[13] Nikos Vafeas concludes, "Senior directors compromise shareholder interests by inflating CEO salaries."

Although extended tenure may be "detrimental to shareholder interests," the Vafeas study also reports no evidence of personal favor gained, such as further directorships or consultancy opportunities.

Our study offers a more positive picture. "We have known each other for a long time. We asked one or two of the non execs to stay on longer than their two terms. They were good and provided the challenge we needed," says the UK CEO, of a large infrastructure company.

The CEO in question refers to, first, his chairman, a nine-year relationship, and second, to certain nonexecutive directors (NEDs) that had contributed a great deal. The point made is that director contribution improves with time. In fact, numerous chairmen, CEOs, and external directors, unwilling to be identified so as not to be seen as undermining governance protocols concurred that a high-performing board is not assisted by limitations to director tenure.

Other comments support the idea that continuity is helpful. "The chemistry is good. That really helps," says one CEO. "We know how to challenge and yet be strongly tied to each other," adds an independent director.

"We are all wary of what will happen, when certain of our key directors retire because of Higgs. It's not a question of finding the skills. It's more of fit and making that real contribution," says a chairman.

The effect of a new director on board dynamics is not sufficiently researched. The delicate balance of chemistry and personalities can so easily be undermined, even with the change of one external director. In the opinion of many, a high performing board requires anything between a 7–12 year period of tenure together.

Dr Bernd Scheifele, CEO and President of Heidelberg Cement, concurs with the extended tenure viewpoint.

"I would say most of the best performing companies in Germany are typically not publicly owned, they are family owned or family controlled. They nominate their people according to performance and what is best in the interest of the company in the long term." Citing differences of company structure, namely the shareholding being in one or a few hands, the message is trust and confidence are built up over extended periods of time.

Bearing in mind that governance protocols and legal requirements have arisen from actual or perceived corporate misbehavior, the policy of limiting board tenure is likely to continue.

Despite public policy, board tenure remains of secondary concern to capability. The contrasting requirements of "fit in" and yet contribute are not easily integrated. The fear of maintaining high quality performance, particularly with changes of key members of the board, is not unfounded. High performing boards do not readily recapture their world-class nature as a result of change of board members. For this reason, if not for any other, attention to succession eases the lows of the learning curve.

Defusing executive remuneration

One of the thorniest issues in the current governance debate is that of executive pay. Warren Buffett is attributed with referring to executive compensation as "the acid test" of US corporate reform. The *Financial Times* highlights: "One of the problems with measuring progress in the field of executive pay is that the gauges used are at best crude, at worst, open to dispute."[14]

Comments the chairman of a South African company: "It depends on a number of factors. We discuss each case, at committee, and then recommendations are put to the board. We compare; we assess; we consider contribution; we also take into account all those factors not visible to the outside world. The whole discussion is really very private."

Few in our study chose to discuss the subject. Of those few, even fewer went into any depth. The topic is sensitive. It is also very public and has received extensive attention from the press.

The very essence of executive remuneration, assessing performance, is open to substantial dispute. Controversy surrounds CEO performance when related to increase in shareholder value and the meeting of shareholder expectations. Analysis of Fortune 500 companies between the years 2000 and 2002 shows revenues down, profits down, and losses up (see Table 7.1).[15]

It is little wonder that the *Financial Times* article reports "disbelief" at a presentation of the Business Roundtable, Washington, United States, which attempted to prove a close link between increases in executive pay and comparable improvements in shareholder returns.[16] The audience was mainly made up of CEOs.

Table 7.1   24 month performance assessment (US$)

	2000	2001	2002
Total revenue	7.2 trillion	7.4 trillion	7.0 trillion
Total profit	443.9 billion	206.2 billion	69.9 billion
Loss	18.1 billion	148.5 billion	2957 billion
Number of companies (loss)	53	97	120

The issue of executive pay is not going to go away. A world-class chairman is one who faces the issue head on – and develops an approach that can be legitimized.

The Economist reports: "Overall, just 37 percent of new pay plans introduced in the past year by Britain's 350 biggest companies used shareholder return as the main measure of performance, down from 47 percent a year earlier."[17]

Incentives capturing medium- to long-term measures of personal and organizational performance are creeping into the boardroom.

One measure that somewhat balances out situational idiosyncrasies is peer comparison. With no reasonably satisfactory mechanism for remunerating the performance of top executives, comparison with the "similar other" is a simple mechanism to fall back on. Its downside is that it is not performance determined. Sometimes positioned as motivational, peer comparison is a hygiene factor – "if you want me to work for you, why are you paying me less than him/her down the road?" The US Business Roundtable has attempted to utilize peer comparison as a worthwhile tool for determining pay. They offer so-called optimal benchmarks. Any CEO who earns more than the Roundtable's, "median compensation" of £6.83 million had better be able to explain how and why.[18]

Despite numerous efforts to better address the vexed issue of executive pay, the *Financial Times* has had to admit: "There seem to be surprisingly few antidotes to this endemic boardroom condition."[19]

Linking executive pay with performance seems the obvious solution. But the three ultimate goals of shareholder value, competitive advantage, and differentiation, sit uncomfortably side by side.

Despite all other innovations, stock options remain a prime lever for linking personal performance with corporate performance. Stock options have attracted comment ranging from concerned critique to plain abuse. The *Financial Times* reports shareholder activists who estimate the pay difference between the average operative against the average CEO in the United States as 300:1.[20] Attracta Lagan and Brian Moran, in their book *3D Ethics*, dispute the comparator as derisory and offer the sum of 4589 times greater than the take-home pay of the average American worker.[21]

The *Wall Street Journal* is particularly vocal in its critique of board handling of stock options.[22] In the traumatic period immediately post–September 11 (2001), a considerable number of companies offered options to their senior executives at considerably depressed prices. The attack on the World Trade Center closed Wall Street for days. The resulting confusion from terrorist attack brought about a stock price fall. The newly reduced options price would remain the same for years into the future.

Wall Street Journal analysis shows how some companies rushed, amid the post–September 11 stockmarket decline – the worst full week for the Dow Jones Industrial Average since Germany invaded France in May 1940 – to give executives especially valuable options. From September 12, 2001, through to the end of that month, 511 top executives of 186 of these companies got stock option grants. The number who received grants was 2–6 times as many in the same stretch of September 2000. Ninety-one companies that didn't regularly grant stock options did so in the first two weeks of trading after the terrorist attack. Their grants were concentrated around September 21 when the market reached its postattack low.

All this begs the question of where fair pay ends and overcompensation begins. Cited is Pfizer's CEO, Hank McKinnell's remuneration: "lump sum retirement benefit for 35 years' service is $83m, or a projected $6.5m in retirement pay per year. That exceeds his

$2.27m salary with a bonus of $3.7m plus options." Shareholders questioned the value gained from their CEO when Pfizer shares dropped by around 43 percent over the recent few years.[23]

Of course, one of the difficulties with linking performance and pay is that the effects on performance of improved operations – whether as a result of restructuring, outsourcing, or introducing new products and equipment – are not instant. There is always a time lag. This makes it extremely difficult to prove a hard and fast relationship between what the CEO did last year and his level of remuneration.

World-class chairmen and boards show the way forward. Who knows whether certain US companies took advantage of the national tragedy, 9/11, to overcompensate their management? Only the boards of those companies know.

Who knows best whether the remuneration package appropriately includes reward for taking charge of long-term change unlikely to be visible for quite some time? Again, only the board of the company knows.

Clearly and openly specifying the reasoning behind any top executive's remuneration, drawing on immediate performance, as well as future gain effects, displays integrity. The politics of remuneration are as important a consideration as the details of the package. The argument put forward by the chairman may not win over all skeptics but at least trust in the chairman that, under the circumstances, the best deal has been put together should remain beyond reproach.

Accountable today and tomorrow

Accountability is a word that is never out of fashion in the best boardrooms. World-class boards try to anticipate the next development – to future proof the company.

CSR and sustainability

We have examined longevity in the previous section in this chapter and concluded it is a critical consideration but uncontroversial.

Sustainability is anything but! Yet, the critical question for chairmen in the coming years is what to do about the governance of sustainability. In particular, the linkages between the business and its role in society need to be better understood.

"For me, corporate social responsibility is not all about the stuff you read," says Lord Dennis Stevenson. He continues:

> It is not a nice consultant report and we're spending 1 percent of our profits on good causes. It is first, believing in what you are doing. Second, it is, having an ethical view as to how you treat people, the stakeholder. Third, insofar as you spend any of your profits doing things in the community, having a clear, explicit strategy for doing it and a very disciplined one. So, in Pearson, not surprisingly, we spend 99 percent of our money in the community on educational projects.

Dennis Stevenson is unapologetic for the fact that spending shareholder funds on activities not directly related to the business is, in itself, wrong, but as a private person, he is active in promoting social causes. Dennis Stevenson takes the Sir Adrian Cadbury line of defining which corporate responsibilities hold stakeholder significance. Our study shows that the Stevenson view is still in the minority.

"The term itself is just ghastly [referring to sustainability]," says the chairman/CEO/president of a US utilities company. "So many different people attach so many different meanings and whatever you do, you get blamed for the interpretation you did not take on board. Yes, we do some charity work. But this still is a business. I say to people, 'I do not break the law. I am very conscious of what I do and, therefore, I am responsible'."

Statistics confirms a sense of growing unease about the morality of the corporate world. For example:

- 72 percent of Americans feel that corporations have too much power over their lives;
- 73 percent of Americans feel that senior executives are paid too much;
- 74 percent of Americans consider that corporations wield too much political influence.[24]

At the same time, the comments of some of those inside the corporate world are worryingly out of synch with other parts of society. The director of a global investment bank comments:

> Investment decisions are dynamic. Each deal is different and you require imagination as well as being practical to make the deal work. Sometimes it takes months to get the deal right, sometimes minutes. Do you really think that anyone takes notice of this CSR stuff? We are doing deals that can change at any moment with people and institutions that just want to make money! CSR does not even enter into our thinking. The only responsibility is get the deal done and, on some occasions, any way you can. CSR is for the compliance department who tell us how to be compliant and so we are. Even they only do it for legal reasons or in order to counter media accusations."

The investment banker in question captures the sentiments of many to the governance of sustainability: what has that got to do with us?

The countermovement is that the corporation is owned by the community. Unlike the Anglo-Americans, the firm in Continental Europe does not hold central status and is a creation of the state. Accordingly, the firm is not a nexus of contracts, but an entity that bears direct responsibility to stakeholders, such as the workforce and the community (local or distant), and to the legacy left to future generations. For so many Continental Europeans, profit without social redistribution and excessive executive remuneration whilst lower level management and staff/operatives are losing their jobs, is morally wrong.

Even then, Continental Europeans hold different views of sustainability and corporate social responsibility (CSR). As we discussed in Discipline 5, Scandinavians and certain sectors of French society take on the social communitarian view. The responsibility for financing a spread of social care provisions for society is through taxation. For the Anglo-American, reaching 70 percent plus tax thresholds is punitive and unimaginable.

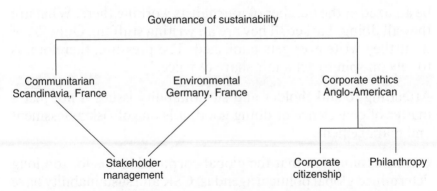

Figure 7.1   Governance of sustainability: a threefold view

The deeply rooted community orientation of Scandinavians and some French is not as strong as with other French or Germans. Despite codetermination laws covering workers' representation on corporate supervisory boards, the corporate responsibility emphasis is on environmental sustainability, a pollution free environment, clean water, clean air, and organic farming (see Discipline 5). The concern is how well the next generation will live. As already outlined, the Brundtland report, the work of the former Norwegian head of state, has set new thinking on environmental standards (Figure 7.1).

The governance of sustainability holds broad meaning. Communitarianism and environmentalism demand sensitive stakeholder management. Taken to extreme, the stakeholder chain could be endless and, thus, overwhelming to address. Contrasting is the Anglo-American philosophy of corporate ethics that unfolded as two governance requirements: ethical corporate citizenship and philanthropy or giving back to society.

No surprise that with such broad scope, sustainability and CSR have become a political hot potato. NGOs, pressure groups, the press, media, and national political parties have leveraged the governance surrounding sustainability for political gain. Vanni Treves, UK Chairman of Korn Ferry, the international search firm, warns of vigilance and ensuring the company has clearly addressed known concerns. He describes a visit to one of the UK's national newspapers, "a huge open plan building. You will be amazed at the number of journalists working there. What are they all doing, I asked? They are all writing stuff up. Only 5% of what they write ever gets published. The pressure, therefore, is to rely on spin to get a fair share of voice."

Attending to stakeholder and sustainability issues is not just a matter of conscience or doing good, it is one of risk assessment and management.

On the assumption that the global corporation has for too long determined global political agendas, CSR and sustainability have been used as tools to rebalance society. What was a movement of concern for the people is now taking on the mantle of political legitimization. The relationship between the firm and society, the role and contribution of the firm, and whether government is shedding its responsibilities on to the private sector are questions left unanswered. What may be unfair is the prospect of political accusation and counterattack increasing in intensity and the firm, as much as government, being in the firing line. What is clear is that CSR and sustainability are here to stay.

The new agenda

The transition from the governance of longevity to that of sustainability is underway. The world's chairmen are at the sharp end of that movement. In future, the world-class chairman will need to be accomplished and at ease with the following:

1. **Fluency in language and meaning**. US and UK executive and nonexecutive directors currently continue to display irritation at the terms sustainability and CSR. Australians focus on health and safety but exhibit little desire to learn more. In contrast, Continental Europeans show deep interest.

"France is the first country in the world that has put the right to live in a healthy environment on the same legal footing as human rights," says the president of a services company in France.

The director went on to recite chapter and verse of human rights legislation and sustainability codes with the same ease as talking sales and marketing. What all this amounts to is that the Anglo-American firm is vulnerable to political attack. Fluency of language of the governance of sustainability counters hostile comment. Even if the board has little desire to become better acquainted with CSR and sustainability, at least speak well, even if you don't mean it! There is little point in attracting unnecessary, damaging comment.

2. **Reputational risk**. The image of the firm is as much an integral aspect of strategy as is merger and acquisition (M&A) or geographic expansion. Minimizing reputational risk does not start with philanthropic notions of good; it starts with scrutiny of one's own home.

Despite SOX, governance codes, and press and media exposure of mal-practice, scandal continues. At the time of writing, the business press is full of reports of improper backdating of executive options, excessive executive pay, and continuing fallout from Hewlett-Packard's boardroom leaks to name just a few.

As we were writing, Hewlett-Packard (HP) was repeatedly in the headlines over boardroom leaks and the role of HP's then chairman, Patricia Dunn, in stemming those leaks. One HP director, Tom Perkins, resigned in protest at the chairman's handling of the case.

Debates rumble on. *The Economist* expresses concern:[25]

> Much of corporate America worries that the crackdown on governance of recent years will create boards full of the great and the good, but with little feel for risk taking or for what makes a company grow. Nowhere is this more feared that on the west coast (USA). Silicon Valley's resistance to improved corporate governance is also affected in the slapdash attitude to accounting for share options that has resulted in the recent backdating scandal, which mostly involves west coast firms.

Our study clearly shows that corporate wrongdoings do not suddenly and unexpectedly hit the headlines. At the levels of chairman, CEO, board and senior management, some insight, even suspicion, exists concerning undesired behavior. We have repeatedly referred to inhibition and the reluctance to raise uncomfortable issues. Nothing grates more with the press and media than expressions of irritation with CSR and taking the high moral ground by proclaiming misuse of shareholder funds for "do-good" projects and then malpractice arises. The firm becomes a prime target for negative press.

The way forward is for the chairman to determine the integrity for the board. The chairman has to do the following:

- strengthen relationships so that uncomfortable issues are raised;
- establish a clear and shared understanding of CSR and sustainability as far as the company is concerned;
- make transparent the manner by which decisions are reached, especially on highly sensitive issues of remuneration and key appointments;
- determine the length and quality of engagement with stakeholders.

Integrity holds powerful meaning for CEOs, chairmen, and board directors alike. As already shown, integrity was the most commonly adopted term to describe the quality of a world-class chairman and a world-class board. Integrity establishes trust. Trust defends reputation. The boundaries of integrity are determined by the chairman. The practice of integrity has to be guaranteed by the chairman.

Thus, whether you like or loathe it, CSR sustainability and reputation are becoming ever more linked. Most in the study acknowledge that being recognized as a great organization requires visible engagement with stakeholders.

"We now have a responsibility committee and I am the chair of that examining the non financial risks to the company. We know that being responsible and displaying our integrity adds a great deal to our reputation," says the president/CEO/chairman of an American insurance corporation.

Again, many confirm that what is in the public domain does not capture the reality of sustainability governance adoption.

"Some firms are getting away with murder. They know how to make themselves look good. Some, like us, are contributing to worthwhile projects and are being publicly battered. We know how to counter the criticism. What is more difficult is making the public and media more aware of what it takes to be responsible, "says the chairman of a US pharmaceutical company.

One disappointing finding of our research is that greater attention to reputational risk has in some cases redirected attention from sustainability and responsibility programs to positive PR projection. Just as CSR is here to stay, so too is investment in looking good.

3. **Sustainability as a business case**. Despite the reaction of a considerable number of US and UK directors that CSR has no place in the boardroom, the same project presented as a business case rapidly increases the attention span of directors.

"Why should I apologise for maximizing shareholder funds, concentrating on the bottom line, being strict on costs and going for profit? That's what I am paid to do. Show me how responsibility causes fit within that brief and I listen," says one US CEO.

In order to attract the attention of the board, position the sustainability project as a business case. The clearer the case, the more seriously the board will consider the case. The more the board backs the project, the greater the interest and disciplined follow through management will show to make it happen. Why? It is because the board has given its full support.

Attracting the right sustainability (or CSR) skills remains a challenge. These are not easy skills to attract on to the board. Few candidates have both accomplished board experience and a sustainability track record. Therefore, the emergence of a new concept, boundary spanning. Researcher Ruth Barratt, explored the boundary spanning challenges of adopting CSR on to the board.[26] Boundary spanning, the exercise of transferring CSR knowledge from one board to another, not only depends on sustainability expertise but also on attitude – the attitude of the board member expert in question to wish to transfer sustainability experience and best practice and also of the board and their willingness to listen. The chairman of a UK retailer speaks thus:

> It took us time to get him. He is also on two other boards but that is ok as we are benefiting. He made it clear we were inattentive to the whole corporate responsibility thing and that could damage us, with investors and also our reputation. Our CEO did not like him at first. He looked down on this CSR stuff but the other non execs said, "No, this is the individual we need." As chairman, I agreed. The learning we are getting from him as a member of our board and through comparing ourselves with the other boards he sits on, is now invaluable.

More enlightened companies share their learning and insights in the corporate responsibility arena. Unfortunately, unlike the chairman of the UK retail organization who welcomed the transfer of learning through the appointment of a CSR specialist on the board, few companies have attempted to improve their portfolio of CSR and sustainability capabilities through boundary spanning.

Having a defensible position on sustainability and CSR issues is critical. As already emphasized, all evidence points to CSR being here for the long term and adopted by particular pressure groups to fulfill their political agenda. The position not to be in is to be labeled as CSR active but to be found inattentive. Clearly state the CSR platform of the organization. It matters less whether the platform is philanthropic, communitarian, environmentally conscious, or that of striving for social improvement through better business performance. Reputation is maintained and competitive advantage gained through action, not promises.

Bad chairmen

The focus of this book has been on what it means to be a good chairman. But, before we close, let us consider what bad chairmen do. Pat Molloy asserts:

> One of the negative things a chairman can do is to become too intrusive and to expect to be involved and kept up to

date on every issue. Servicing the chairman becomes a job in itself and does not add value. The chairman is too close to detail, isn't standing back and taking the higher level view, looking at strategy from the right perspective.

"Bad chairmen come in different packages," says John Phillips. "Some are very dominant people with fixed ideas and want to bull doze everything through and don't encourage debate. The other is one who believes that their sole mission in life is to support the chief executive. It is bad to have a chairman and a board dominated by the chief executive."

Our study emphatically shows that bad chairmen nurture bad boards. Being overintrusive, wanting too much detail, not being strategic, "bulldozing" through fixed ideas, reducing dialogue, and the other extreme, being over subservient; Pat Molloy and John Phillips capture most of the list of descriptions of bad chairmen. A few more are having poor insight, wanting the limelight, talking over others, and just simply being egoistic.

The ultimate test

What does a world-class chairman look like? In part, it is the continuous display of the necessary skills and capabilities, establishing clear roles, achieving shared strategic understanding, robust challenge, influencing skills, and projecting integrity through living one's own and the organization's values. In part, it is the development of self and others.

How is it achieved? By entering into deep consideration of what is meant by world class – for the organization, for the board, and for the CEO and chairman. According to context, the meaning of world class varies considerably. It can mean strategic positioning to gain competitive advantage, determining how to stand apart and be different, displaying how the center adds value, and adopting a governance practice that simultaneously protects and grows the business. All require continuous revisiting. When all that is attended to, it is ultimately being recognized as standing above. In the final analysis, part of it is down to the quality of the people themselves.

"You need to give yourself space and time to reflect, come back and revisit the original question and decision," says Viscount Etienne Davignon. Adds Don Argus:

> The CEO must want the relationship with the board, then the company will start to work extremely well. It's an open, trusting relationship. Now, if you have problems, then you've got to deal with them quickly. You've got to get the 'elephant' out of the room very quickly because it will sap the energy of the organization and once you start sapping the energy, you will not get the performance that company could achieve.

From reflection to action, Viscount Davignon, Tom Sawyer, and Don Argus all make relevant comment. The chairman's role in pushing for the appropriate way forward is now more significant than ever.

Outstanding chairmen create extraordinary boards. Such chairmen are repeatedly described as follows:

- evidence driven;
- always of help – *helping me, as the CEO to be uplifted* (comment from a CEO);
- *helping me think* (comment from an MD);
- *helping me see the bigger picture* (comments from CEOs; NEDs; independent directors);
- clear on the values of the organization.

The ultimate test of the world-class chairman and world-class board is to just ask those directly involved what are this board and its leader really like?

As one independent director put it: "A good board is a good chairman."

Any other business? Contact the authors.

Introduction   The rise, fall, and rise of the chairman

1. All quotations are from research interviews unless otherwise stated.
2. For further information on the role of the board, read B. Garratt (2003), *The Fish Rots from the Head: The Crisis in Our Boardrooms*, London: Profile.
3. The UK model, while much closer to the US model, is more influenced by its European neighbors. Despite sharing a shareholder value philosophy and single tier board structure, the role of chairman in the United States and that in the United Kingdom are substantially different from one another. Role duality, namely the chairman and CEO (and president) being one and the same person, typifies the US corporation, while role separation predominates in British companies.
4. See the semantics of governance literatures. Board members have been identified as *institutional agents*. Management have been termed *corporate agents*. Institutional agents (boards) monitor corporate agents (managers) in order to safeguard investors and provide attractive opportunities for investors. Management serve shareholder (investor) interests and maximize the value of the firm's shareholdings.
5. The Blue Ribbon Committee was established by the New York Stock Exchange and the National Association of Securities Dealers in the United States.

Discipline 1   Delineating boundaries

1. CNN Money.com, "Companies splitting CEO, chairman roles," January 31, 2007.
2. For further information on the chairman-CEO relationship, read A. Kakabadse, N. Kakabadse, and R. Barratt (2006), "Chairman and chief executive officer (CEO): that sacred and secret relationship," *Journal of Management Development*, 25(2), pp. 134–150.
3. For further information on discretionary leadership, see A. Kakabadse and N. Kakabadse (1999), *Essence of Leadership*, London: International Thomson.
4. Quoted in John Gray, "Who's the boss?," *Canadian Business*, 79 (21), pp. 15, 213, IC, October 23, 2006.

5. For further information on vision and visioning, see N. Kakabadse, A. Kakabadse, and L. Lee-Davies (2005), "Visioning the pathway: a leadership process model," *European Management Journal*, 23(2), pp. 237–246.
6. For a pragmatic view of the role of chairman, read the Australian Institute of Company Directors (2006), Chairman of the Board: A Role in the Spotlight, AICD.
7. *Financial Times* (2006), "Ford perfect: ex-newsreader bags Sainsbury's role", May 3, p. 1.

Discipline 2   Sense making

1. For further information on strategy analysis, see K. Ward, C. Bowman, and A. Kakabadse (2005), *Designing World Class Corporate Strategies*, Oxford: Elsevier/Heinemann.
2. I. Bickerton (2006), "Boer to review Ahold strategy," *Financial Times*, May 11, p. 28.
3. For further information on the sales/marketing debate, see A. Kakabadse (1991), *The Wealth Creators: Top People, Top Teams and Executive Best Practice*, London: Kogan Page.
4. Susanne Craig (2006), "Goldman chief takes on firms critics, challenges," *Wall Street Journal: Money and Investing*, April 26, p. 17.

Discipline 3   Interrogating the argument

1. A. Lashinsky (2006), "The Hurd way: how a sales-obsessed CEO rebooted HP," *Fortune*, 153(7), pp. 83–88, April 17.
2. Ibid.
3. Ibid.
4. For further information on dialogue, Plato and Socrates, read: N. Kakabadse and A. Kakabadse (2003), "Polylogue as a platform for governance: integrating people, the planet, profit and posterity," *Corporate Governance: The International Journal of Business in Society*, 3(1), pp. 5–38.
5. "London calling: Macquarie Bank. The Heady climb of an unusual investment bank" (2005), *Economist* 377(8998), p. 105, October 15.
6. Ibid.

Discipline 4   Influencing outcomes

1. For further information on dialectics, the history of dialectics, and the philosopher Habermas, see N. Kakabadse, A. Kakabadse, and K. Kalu (2007), "Communicative action through collaborative inquiry: journey

of a facilitating co-inquirer," *Systemic Practice and Action Research*, available at http://dx.doi.org/10.1007/s11213-006-9061-1, accessed Jan 31, 2007.

Discipline 5   Living the values

1. J. Croft and P.T. Larsen (2006), "Santander sees Abbey financial markets arm as area for growth," *Financial Times*, Week 19, Thursday, May 11, p. 19.
2. For further information on how messages are transmitted in the organization, read A. Kakabadse and N. Kakabadse (1999), *Essence of Leadership*, London: International Thomson, Chapters 5 and 8, particularly p. 328.
3. Table 5.2 is adapted from A. Kakabadse and N. Kakabadse (1999), *Essence of Leadership*, London: International Thomson, Table 8.8, p. 329.
4. For further information on the Enron case and the position adopted by the various parties, read S. McNulty (2006), Enron case hangs in the balance as jury retires, *Financial Times*, Thursday, May 18, p. 26; S. Foley (2006), Enron chairman takes stand to tell of an "American nightmare," *The Independent Business*, Tuesday, April 25, p. 42.
5. For a further, recent reading of Adam Smith's *The Wealth of Nations*, see A. Smith (1991), *The Wealth of Nations*, London: Everyman's Library.
6. J. Bentham (1787/1995), *The Panopticon Writings* (ed. M. Bozovi) and J.S. Mill (1895/1947), *Liberty and Representative Government*, London: JM Dent.
7. I. Kant (1788/2004), *Critique of Pure Reason* (translated by JMD Meiklejohn), New York: Dover Publications.
8. For further information on Howard Bowen, read H.R. Bowen (1953), *Social Responsibilities of the Businessman*, New York: Harper & Row.
9. G.H. Brundtland (1987), *Our Common Future: The World Commission on Environment and Development*, Oxford: Oxford University Press.
10. For further information on Matthew Bishop's views, read M. Salls (2004), "An opposing view on corporate social responsibility," *Harvard Business School, Working Knowledge*, available at http://hbswk.hbs.edu, accessed June 9, 2004.
11. For further information on excessive executive pay in the USA, see Executive Excess at www.executiveexcess.com. Also refer to A. Lagan and B. Moran (2006), "3D ethics personal, corporate, social: implementing work place value?" *Content Management Pty Ltd.*, Maleny, Queensland, Australia.

Discipline 6   Developing the board

1. For further information on the Richard Leblanc paper, read R. Leblanc (2005), "Assessing board leadership," *Corporate Governance*, 13 (5), pp. 654–666.

2. For further information on the Mercer Delta publication on boards and board performance, see D.A. Nadler, B.A. Behan, and M.B. Nadler (eds.) (2006), *Building Better Boards,* San Francisco, CA: Jossey Bass, Wiley Imprints.
3. Murray Steele, of Cranfield, accepted the challenge of redesigning director development and now offers one of the few programs in the world where each director's ways of thinking and doing are put to the test.
4. For further information on Paul Myners, see P. Myners (2006), "Pick the bankers rather than the bank they work for," *Financial Times, Special Report, Corporate Finance*, "The Good Guide to Selecting Investment Banks," *Financial Times, Special Report, Corporate Finance*, Wednesday, June 28, p. 5.
5. *The Economist* (2006), "That tricky first 100 days," *The Economist*, Executive On-boarding Business, July 15, p. 72.
6. Ibid.
7. For further information on the Transition Curve, see Kubler-Ross, E. (1969), *On Death and Dying*, London: Macmillan.

On being world class
The six disciplines at work

1. For further information on diplomats' placement in the private sector, see D. Doombey, R. Sullivan, and J. Willman (2006), "Diplomats hired by blue chip groups," *Financial Times, Foreign Office*, Friday, September 15, p. 3.
2. For further information on chairmen, succession, see C. Grande and K. Burgess (2006), "Boards don't like to talk about it. Chairmen Succession," *Financial Times, Companies UK*, Tuesday, August 29, p. 20.
3. For further information on the need for formal succession planning, see K. Burgess and C. Grande (2006), "A more formal planning process is needed," *Financial Times, Companies UK*, Tuesday, August 29, p. 20.
4. Refer to K. Burgess and C. Grande (2006), "A more formal planning process is needed," *Financial Times, Companies UK*, Tuesday, August 29, p. 20.
5. For further information on the speech of Sir Adrian Cadbury presented to the 7th International Conference on Corporate Governance organized by the World Council for Corporate Governance in London, May 11–12, 2006, see Sir A. Cadbury (2006), "Widening role of corporate governance," *Corporate Governance: International Journal for Enhancing Board Performance*, 6 (3), pp. 5–6.
6. H. Donker and S. Zahir (2008), "Towards an impartial and effective corporate governance rating system," *Corporate Governance: The International Journal of Business in Society*, 8 (1), January, forthcoming.

7. For further information on Sarbanes–Oxley, see B. Jopson (2006), "Deadline on Sarbanes–Oxley closing. Accounting standards," *Financial Times*, National News Business and Economy, Monday, July 10, p. 3.

8. Ibid.

9. Ibid.

10. Also B. Jopson (2006), "Pain blamed on US red tape zealots eager to tick boxes. Accounting Standards," *Financial Times,* National News Business and Economy, Monday, July 10, p. 3.

11. Ibid.

12. Ibid.

13. For further information on the effects of board tenure, see N. Vafeas (2003), "Length of board tenure on outside director independence," *Journal of Business Finance and Accounting*, 20(7 and 8), September/October, pp. 1043–1064.

14. The Warren Buffet comment is taken from A. Hill (2006), "Pay and the boardroom benchmark," *Financial Times,* Monday, July 10, p. 17.

15. For further information on company performance, see A. Kakabadse, N. Kakabadse, and A. Jarman (2006), "The American State and the Corporation: The Case for Governance Intervention," in N. Kakabadse and A. Kakabadse, *Governance, Strategy and Policy: Seven Critical Essays*, Basingstoke: Palgrave Macmillan, p. 123.

16. A. Hill (2006); ibid., 17.

17. For further information on executive pay assessment and the reports from Deloitte, Touche, Tohmatsu, see *The Economist* (2006), "Lowering the bar: executive pay," *The Economist*, No. 379/8478, May 20, pp. 31–32.

18. A. Hill (2006); ibid., 17.

19. A. Hill (2006); ibid., 17.

20. A. Hill (2006); ibid., 17.

21. For further information on the pay differences between CEOs and operatives, see A. Lagan and B. Moran (2006), *3D ethics: personal, corporate, social: implementing workplace values*, Content Management Pty Ltd, Maleny, Queensland, Australia, p. 32.

22. For further information on the US stock options 'scandal' post–September 11, see C. Forelle, J. Bandler, and M. Maremont (2006), "Executive pay: The September 11 factor in timing of stock options," *The Wall Street Journal*, Tuesday, July 19, pp. 14–15.

23. For further information on Pfizer's CEO pay and the questions it has raised, see C. Bowe (2006), "Pfizer Chief's Pay Scrutinised," *Financial Times*, Companies in America, Thursday, April 27, p. 26.

24. For further information on corporate influence and inequality, see A. Kakabadse and N. Kakabadse (2001), *The Geo Politics of Governance: The Impact of Contrasting Philosophies*, New York: Palgrave, Chapter 2, p. 75.

25. HP's spying story continued with, *The Economist* (2006), "Hewlett Packard: East versus West, in Silicon Valley, HP's crisis rambles on," *The Economist*, September 30, p. 84.
26. For further information on boundary spanning, see R. Barratt (2005), "The role and contribution of the non executive director: implications for corporate social responsibility in the boardroom," PhD Thesis, Cranfield University.

INDEX

[Page numbers in **bold** denote those containing tables and *italics* denote those containing figures. Note cues numbers are preceded by an indication for the relevant chapter number, e.g. 203n.I.3 denotes note cue number 3 for the introduction chapter]